You find them everywhere: tripping down the front steps at school, dribbling their food at the lunch table, taking a face shower at the water fountain, getting lost in a darkened aisle at the movie theatre—GOONS! Maybe you're even one of them! If you are, don't worry; help is on the way. If you think you're not, better go ask your friends. Everyone is a goon at one time or another.

But nobody wants to be a goon...

How Not to Be a Goon is a book designed to help you polish down the rough edges—not only on the outside but also on the inside where God sees them. Author Doug Fields (goon expert for the LIGHT FORCE) shares great ideas—from the Bible and his experience as a youth leader—that will help you mature and become the kind of person you've always wanted to be. Topics include: integrity, affirming others, competition, nonverbal communication, meekness, humor, cliques, personal reflection, happiness, managing conflicts, and many others.

HOW NOT TO BE A GOON

Great Ideas About Growing Up

BY DOUG FIELDS

Regal Books

A Division of GL Publications
Ventura, California, U.S.A.

Illustrations
by
Rick Bundschuh

Rights for publishing this book in other languages are contracted by Gospel Literature International (GLINT) foundation. GLINT also provides technical help for the adaptation, translation, and publishing of Bible study resources and books in scores of languages worldwide. For further information, contact GLINT, Post Office Box 488, Rosemead, California, 91770, U.S.A., or the publisher.

©Copyright 1986 by Regal Books
Published by Regal Books
A Division of GL Publications
Ventura, California 93006
Printed in U.S.A.

Library of Congress Cataloging in Publication Data

Fields, Doub, 1962-
    How not to be a goon.

    Includes bibliographies.
    1. Conduct of life.   I. Title.
BJ1581.2.F53   1986   248.8'3   86-17679
ISBN 0-8307-1160-0

1 2 3 4 5 6 7 8 9 10 / 91 90 89 88 87 86

Dedication

To Jim and Marge Fields, my loving parents, whose unconditional love and acceptance has never failed me.

SPECIAL THANKS TO:

Jim Burns—who has always believed in me and taught
me much of the material in this book.
Mike Driggs—for showing me what Christianity is all
about and showing me it's okay to fail.
Cathy—my wife, whose loving encouragement,
patience, and advice brought reality to the pages of
this book.

Table of Contents

1
INTEGRITY:
The Pursuit of Truth
15

2
ENTHUSIASM:
The Magic of Happiness
27

3
CONFLICT MANAGEMENT:
The Tough Road to Better Relationships
37

4
COMPETITION:
Do You Always Have to Win?
47

5
GIVING:
The Percentage Game
57

6
TRANSPARENCY:
An Open Window to Better Relationships
67

7
AFFIRMATION:
The Life-Changing Power of Words
75

8
NONVERBAL COMMUNICATION:
What You Don't Say Speaks Loudly
85

9
MEEKNESS:
Gentle and Strong
97

10
CLIQUES:
Why You Should Become a Clique Buster
105

11
LAUGHTER:
Add Joy to Your Life
113

12
REFLECTION:
Taking Time to Know God and Yourself
125

Foreword

I'm a goon! I feel a lot better now that I've gotten that off my chest. I'm also in the long process of becoming less of a goon—you are too just by the mere fact that you are reading this book.

A goon is someone who hasn't mastered the qualities that there are in this life. You see, there are many qualities that are good for us to have. In this book I've written on only twelve that can help us to become better people and servants of Christ. What's very interesting about these qualities is that they are rarely, if ever, taught in the church. The church, in general, expects that when we become Christians we will automatically receive these qualities like we receive God's Spirit. This just doesn't happen!

Expectations are placed upon us as Christians to be quality people. Realistically all that should be expected of us is that we are filled with God's love. In reality we are just Christian goons. We have got to learn these qualities and with God's help we will become less of a goon and more like Christ.

I pray that the qualities in this book will help you become a more quality Christian so that your love and interaction with others will cause them to know that you aren't a goon but God's disciple because of the love you have for other people.

Read with a desire to grow and join the long, painful yet rewarding journey of becoming less of a goon and more like Christ.

Trying not to be a goon,

Doug Fields
Newport Beach, CA

INTEGRITY

The Pursuit of Truth

One of my lifelong goals is to be known as a man of integrity. The word integrity can be thought of as synonymous with such terms as honesty, trustworthiness, loyalty and faithfulness. Today someone who possesses these character qualities is indeed to be admired. (And yes it is possible for golfers and fishermen to be people of integrity.) The specific quality of integrity that seems most difficult to obtain is honesty.

Most of us are faced daily with decisions that require us to choose between right and wrong, telling the truth or lying, or deciding whether or not to keep a secret. These decisions can be hard; especially since we live in a society of declining morals and standards.

Just yesterday I was faced with three decisions that forced me to draw upon my growing well of integrity. Early in the morning an organization called me and told me they were going to send me a check for $1,485 since I had sent them a check for $1,500 instead of $15. After quickly looking at my records I found out that they were wrong. They had posted the wrong amount—to my advantage. For a few brief moments I thought about how nice it would be to have the extra cash in my pocket. Since they made the mistake I would probably be able to live with myself and not feel too much guilt. I even thought of the computer that I had been lusting over, the one that was way out of my price range. How nice it would be to write my books on that machine. Maybe it was to be a "gift" from the Lord! (I doubt it.)

Later, when I left the house I found that my car had been broken into and my stereo had been stolen. After calling my insurance agency I was told that all they wanted was a breakdown of what had been stolen and they would reimburse me. I thought, "Hey, I could say that there were all kinds of things in the car that actually weren't there and add a couple hundred dollars to the price of the stereo and they would never know." I tried to justify my thoughts by saying to myself that I had been ripped off so why not rip off someone else? It would have been easy to do.

That same evening my wife, Cathy, and I went to a theater and saw an early showing of a great movie. When it was over we bumped into some friends in the lobby and talked with them for awhile when they invited us to slip into the movie that they were about to see. This was another hard decision to make. Since we didn't pay for the second movie, it would be stealing if we did walk in. Again it would have been so easy since there was no one there taking tickets.

Take a minute to think of all the daily decisions that you have to make that deal with honesty. They are not always easy and we don't always make the right choices. I know I don't! Like yesterday, I blew it on one of the decisions I was faced with. I felt badly afterwards since I knew beforehand that what I was going to do was wrong. It wasn't worth it! Guilt has to be one of the worst feelings! Plus the second movie was not even as good as the first one. Even though it can be hard to make the right decisions I really believe that as Christians we need to pursue Christ's example.

JESUS SPEAKS OUT ON INTEGRITY

Jesus speaks loudly for integrity in Matthew 5:37: "Let your 'Yes' be 'Yes,' and your 'No,' 'No.'" In other words, speak the truth so others can trust and believe in your words.

The first time I understood this verse I set out to see how many times I *did not* speak the truth in one day. I was amazed at the results (and I am no different from most of you). I would see one of my friends at school and say, "Hey is that a new shirt? It looks great!" Yet in the back of my mind I would be thinking, "That is the ugliest shirt I have ever seen!" Or I would say, "I would really like to come to your party but my grandparents are flying in from Colorado" knowing the entire time that I really did not want to go to the party. I was continually catching myself trying to find ways around the truth. This has been a struggle of mine for a long time.

I've been helped in my struggle by a system. When Cathy and I got married we "installed" an integrity beeper that would help us hold each other accountable in our pursuit of being people of integrity. Every time either one of us would slip and say or do something that was not honest the other person would make a beep sound to help remind us that we had fallen short. For example, I might say, "McSunas, thanks for dropping over; it was good to spend time with you" and Cathy would beep because she knew McSunas had come by at a terrible time when I really needed to get something done. We have a lot of fun with this little game and it really helps to remind us when we fall from the truth. (Unfortunately Cathy beeps much more than I do.)

I believe that many of us struggle with integrity. There's a good chance we have not adequately dealt with this common problem. In this chapter we will look at the results of lacking integrity and at some realistic steps that we can take to help us to be the honest men and women that God intends for us to be:

> But the man who lives by the truth comes out into the light, so that it may be plainly seen that what he does is done in God. (John 3:21, *JB*)

RESULTS OF LACKING INTEGRITY

Lies Bring on Unwanted Guilt

As Christians, when we are dishonest, and know that we have done wrong, we usually feel guilty. Guilt is a powerful feeling that seems to somehow invade our lives and cause us to feel like we are worthless. We live with this guilt not knowing what to do with it. Guilt is like a tiny person inside us. Every time we do something wrong this person reminds us of our wrong by beating up our insides, causing great pain. There are many different opinions as to why we experience guilt, but the cold, hard fact is that we do and it can be an emotional, spiritual, and even physical drain on who we are as God's people.

Lies Lead to Trouble

Some of us get in trouble because we cannot remember all the lies we have told and who we have told them to. When I was in high school I knew of a guy who actually kept a small note pad with him at all times trying to record his lies so he could remember who he had told what. His little system did not work and he jeopardized his relationships because his friends found out that they had been lied to for a long time. Even with the latest computer systems it would be an incredible chore to try to file all of your lies just so you would not get caught. It just wouldn't be worth it!

I learned very early that lies have a way of catching up with us. I once told my parents that I was going to spend the night at Bob King's house and Bob told his parents that he was going to spend the night at my house. We then took small lounge chairs and jumped the fence of a nearby drive-in movie where we were going to spend most of our evening. Before the first picture was over we bumped into Bob's older brother and quickly made up the story that we were there with my parents. After the movie was over we went to sleep in our new fort near the riverbed so we could get up early in the morning for the best fishing. When we returned to our own homes later the next day we were confronted by our parents, who acted as though they didn't know what was going on. We each told our own little lie about the great time we had at the other friend's home. Little did we know that the night before Bob's older brother called to ask my older sister a question; and you can guess how things progressed from that point! We had told so many different lies that Bob and I could not even remember the real story. I would have rather been anywhere in the world instead of where I was, trying to get my way out of that mess. Dishonesty has a way of getting us in trouble no matter how smart we think we are.

> Lies will get any man into trouble, but honesty
> is its own defense. (Prov. 12:13, *TLB*)

We Begin to Believe Lies

I have found in dealing with people who have trouble telling the truth that they actually begin to believe their lies as if they were really true. The person who lies creates a false mask which keeps him or her from being the real person God created. Behind this mask is someone who, for whatever reason, began telling lies and was not able to escape the trouble that lies bring and was forced to continue the lies that become so much a part of his or her life. The compulsive liar actually cannot tell if they are telling the truth or not. People who lie compulsively and who no longer know whether or not they are telling the truth are called *pathological liars:* They have an emotional problem. Do you know someone like this? Could you possibly be this someone?

Christians are not immune to lying. But the Christian, on the road to maturity should make integrity a quality of his or her life. But don't be surprised if you or another Christian has a problem with lying. Like other qualities, conquering lying is a process for the Christian.

Don't tell lies to each other; it was your old life with all its wickedness that did that sort of thing; now it is dead and gone. You are living a brand new kind of life that is continually learning more and more of what is right, and trying constantly to be more and more like Christ who created this new life within you. (Col. 3:9,10, *TLB*)

Lying Affects Others

Oftentimes when we tell lies we are doing so to look good or to save us from some type of pain or trouble. We rarely think of the incredible consequences that others feel when they somehow become involved in our lies. Friends may wind up lying to help protect our original lie just because they cherish our friendship. I would go as far as to say that many of us might even expect a true friend to lie for us. I once heard a story of a young boy who was told by his mother to answer the phone and tell whoever it was that she was in the bathtub and couldn't come to the phone. So the little boy quickly answered the phone and said, "We don't have a bathtub but that's where Mom is."

Another way in which we affect others with our speech is by carelessly talking about them. We call this gossip. The effect that it can have on another person's life is unbelievable! I have seen people emotionally destroyed and relationships broken simply because someone decided to talk about another person with distorted facts. The Bible goes as far as saying that "Telling lies about someone is as harmful as hitting him with an axe, or wounding him with a sword, or shooting him with a sharp arrow" (Prov. 25:18, *TLB*).

We like to be "people of the know" who are up on the latest gossip. One of your friends may hear something about someone and relay that information to you. Now that you have the information you will most likely judge the person who was the subject of the gossip because you think that what you heard is truth. Gossip is like getting five pieces to a 100 piece puzzle and then judging the beauty of the puzzle by only those five pieces. It is

23

terrible! Yet many people gossip daily. As you may know, it is a horrible sight to see one of your friends destroyed because they have been talked about unfairly.

STEPS LEADING TO INTEGRITY

Even after reading the results of lacking integrity it can still be difficult to be men and women of integrity. It becomes increasingly hard to be honest when we feel that the truth will make us look bad, or when the lie is so small that we believe we will never get caught, or even when we think that there is no way we will get by without being dishonest.

I believe with all my heart that there is a road to recovery if you struggle in this area as many of us do.

Admit Your Problem

One of the first steps to overcoming a lack of integrity is to admit to yourself that you have a problem; you are no better than other Christians who struggle with this common fault. I have counseled many students who are unwilling to admit that they may have a problem. Many feel that by confessing they are "lowering" themselves and that they are going to look bad. My opinion, is that this mentality (not wanting to look bad) is the reason for the problem in the first place.

It takes a strong person to be able to admit a failing! Just recently, Cindy, a girl in my youth group would not admit to herself that she had a problem with drinking and drugs. She would come home at least three times a week either drunk or stoned but was still unable to convince herself she had a problem.

One night at 3:30 A.M. Cindy called me and asked me if I could come pick her up. When I arrived at the house where she was partying, I found her passed out on the bathroom floor lying in her own vomit. The next morning she told me she was ready to admit her problem and wanted help. As I write, Cindy is in a drug rehabilitation hospital recovering from the sickness that was a part of her life. Her God-given life is being changed forever because she was strong enough to admit she had a problem.

Would you be as willing as Cindy to admit that you have a problem? What if that problem is in the area of honesty or integrity?

Ask Someone to Hold You Accountable

If you have a problem with honesty and you are ready to admit it to yourself, it is helpful to share your concern with a friend. He or she can help you be accountable in your pursuit of integrity. I know first hand how hard this is to do!

Who knows and spends time with you? Ask him or her to help you use the integrity beeper system that Cathy and I use. It is really a helpful reminder! (In the Transparency chapter we talk about how it is nice to have a friend with whom you can share anything, even your faults.)

Ask God for Truth

God is the source of truth. If we want truth to illuminate our lives, we need to go to God through Jesus, and He promises us we will find it. Jesus said, "I am the way and the truth and the life. No one comes to the Father except through me" (John 14:6). Ask God to be a vital part in the process of pursuing integrity. Pray constantly and know that He is hearing your prayers. He wants you to be a mature Christian. Jesus said, "I came to bring truth to the world. All who love the truth are my followers" (John 18:37, *TLB*).

You Are in a Process

Throughout this entire book I will constantly remind you that this life with Jesus called Christianity is a process. You will not wake up tomorrow a person without faults. Do not be discouraged if you are trying to be a person of integrity and you find yourself failing at times. This is natural!

One of my favorite book titles is *Three Steps Forward, Two Steps Back*. This is the Christian life in a nutshell. We try to do better and move three steps forward then we fail and move two steps back but we gain one step in the process. The exciting fact is that one step is one step closer to maturity in Christ. Keep stepping towards integrity!

ENTHUSIASM

The Magic of Happiness

There is true magic in the life of someone who is enthusiastic. I love being around enthusiastic people; they have such a positive outlook on life. They make me want to be enthusiastic too. I just love it! Yet as I go through life, I study people's faces and what I see is a lot of depression, loneliness and hiding behind layers of skin. Sure, I see smiles and hear laughter, but it is a rare moment when I come across someone who bubbles with the magic gift of enthusiasm. This person vividly stands out in the crowd (not like the person who is obnoxious or wild), and seems to wear a glowing radiation.

Just imagine for a second what it would be like if we were all to wear neon signs above our heads that flashed sentences describing our lives. The enthusiastic person would have a sign that flashed: "I love life," "Isn't it great to be alive!" or "Life is a blast." On the other hand, there are some students in my youth group whose signs would read: "Oh well, I guess it is another day," "There is nothing to do," "I don't care" or "I'm bored." What would your sign say?

Regardless of where you stand on the enthusiasm scale, there is plenty of room to grow. In this chapter we will look at what enthusiasm can do for us and then we will look at how we can become more enthusiastic people.

WHAT ENTHUSIASM CAN DO FOR YOU

Enthusiasm Is Contagious

When we are around enthusiastic people we tend to become enthusiastic; it is as simple as that.

When I was in college I took a class called 'Recreation and Camping.' The reason I took this class was because it sounded easy and since it was at the dreadful hour of 8:00 A.M., I could sleep in and probably not miss much material.

I went the first day of class to pick up the course outline and see what the class offered. As I sat in the cold, moist room with fifteen other yawning students, I tried to figure out what the class would be like since no one knew the professor. Then this big man pranced in with a smile larger than my desk. He walked (it was really more of a gallop than a walk) straight toward me; I'll never forget it. He stuck his long, wide hand in front of me and said, "Good morning! My name is Wayne Tesch, my friends call me Wayne!"

"Hi, my name is Doug Fields," I said as I began to slowly move up in my seat.

"Doug, I'm thrilled you are in this class!" Wayne then went to each of the other students and repeated that same opening line.

You should have seen how the atmosphere of that classroom changed! His enthusiasm was contagious! All of our eyes were glued to him as he gave his introductory speech. If he had had a neon sign his enthusiasm would have overloaded it!

I never missed one of his classes, I actually brought friends to this 8:00 A.M. class (which wasn't easy). I'd say,

"You have got to see this guy, he makes school and learning fun; it is unbelievable!" His enthusiasm changed my life as well as the whole class. Enthusiasm is definitely contagious!

Enthusiasm Helps Us to Reach Goals

My friend Jim Burns has said for years, "He who aims at nothing gets there every time." I believe in this as well as the power behind goal setting. If you are a goal setter (and I would encourage you to be one) then you are always trying to figure out the best steps to reaching your goals.

Enthusiasm should always be one of your first steps. If you are excited about reaching your goal then there is little that can stop you if it is a realistic goal. Enthusiasm can be a great motivator. I would like to rewrite Jim's quote and say, "He who aims with enthusiasm gets there every time." Charles M. Schwab, one of the dynamic men who built the American industrial structure, once said, "A man can succeed at almost anything for which he has unlimited enthusiasm."[1] Enthusiasm can help you reach your goals.

Enthusiasm Attracts People

This fact is sure true in my life! Like I said, I love being around enthusiastic people! I am attracted to those who have that magic of enthusiasm. Who are the people you really like to be around or would like to be around if you could? What is it you like about them? Most likely they are positive people who are enthusiastic about life. Enthusiasm seems to have magnetic capabilities that quickly attracts others.

When my friend Donna Gibson started dating David (now her husband), who she had been interested in for some time, we got together for lunch to talk about her new relationship. I asked her every question I could think of, expressing my interest in her new relationship. When she responded I would eagerly and sincerely listen with enthusiasm while I mentally formulated another question. I was excited for Donna and the new things that were happening in her life.

After lunch she told me how very thankful she was that I was so excited and interested in what she was doing. That lunch was a positive boost in our friendship because ever since she has told me of all her new and exciting adventures. Enthusiasm brought our friendship closer together.

Enthusiasm Sells

The best salesmen and women in the world are those who not only believe in their product but are enthusiastic about it. Would you buy something from someone who said, "You wouldn't want to buy this— would you?" We buy from confident and enthusiastic people.

When I was in Little League I had to sell candy bars to earn a uniform. I had to sell fifty overpriced, high calorie candy bars. My plan was to go to twenty-five houses and sell two bars per house. Then the uniform would be mine!

Well, I sure learned a hard lesson. After twenty-five houses, I had sold only one bar (to my best friend's mom). I stumbled to my house crying and planning to quit Little League since I would be the only one without a uniform.

After my parents picked me up off the floor, they asked me to tell them my sales pitch. I really didn't have one, I just went up to the door, grunted a little bit, held the candy bar out, and raised my eyebrows as if to say, "You wouldn't want these candy bars would you?" After hearing this, my dad went to find a tape recorder while my mom helped me write a surefire speech. Then I practiced the speech into the recorder and in front of the mirror, throwing in smiles and accenting my words with enthusiastic voice inflections and gestures. I was good! Later, my parents stood at the front door and watched me race down the street to attack the neighborhood once again. Nineteen houses later (count 'em—nineteen) I raced back to my house empty-handed with my pockets holding the money for my new uniform.

Enthusiasm helps to sell not only products but also yourself. Enthusiasm helps when interviewing for a job, making first impressions, and when you want to get a message across to another person.

Enthusiasm Can Change Your Life

I have already listed four specific life changing features of enthusiasm and I know there are many more. Enthusiasm can: change or help your attitude, build confidence, relieve fears, help you with a job or school work, make you a better athlete, help you appreciate life more, bring you closer to God and much, much more.

If I have helped you see some of the exciting things enthusiasm can do for you, then read on to see how you can become a more enthusiastic person. If you still aren't sold on enthusiasm, you may need to start this chapter over again.

HOW TO BECOME ENTHUSIASTIC

Start and End Each Day with an Enthusiastic Attitude

This is the day the Lord has made, let us rejoice and be glad in it." (Ps. 118:24)

If we could copy these words of the psalmist and place them in our hearts we would surely become more enthusiastic people. Each morning when you wake up repeat this verse as an expectation of a great day. Also, before you go to bed thank God for the day you have been given and pray that you might wake with an enthusiasm about life and an excitement for the God who created your day.

Think Enthusiastically

Your mind is an incredible gift from God that holds the potential of helping you to be the person God intended you to be. In your mind visualize yourself being an enthusiastic person. After you pray for your day, picture all the people you may see, the conversations you will have, and places you will go. Then imagine yourself being enthusiastic throughout the day as you interact with what God has planned for you. You will find that you will be drawn to what your mind has pictured. Try it out, I do it all the time. God gave us minds, so why not use them to help us be more enthusiastic people?

Do Not Overload Your Life

I am writing out of weakness rather than strength in this area. I know first hand that it is hard to be enthusiastic when you are burnt-out. I have a girl in my youth group who is on the swim team, drill team, takes dance lessons, is involved in school government, teaches Sunday School, has a part-time job, goes to church, and is part of our high school leadership on top of her normal school load. Her parents came to me wondering why she is lethargic in relationships and around the house. They need to open their eyes to the fact that their daughter is burning herself out and has no time to be enthusiastic.

It seems to me that tiredness and enthusiasm are two opposite extremes. For enthusiasm to be a vital part of your everyday life you may need to prioritize some of the events in your life so that you leave some untapped energy that can be coal to an enthusiastic fire.

Enthusiasm Comes When You Are Connected to God

The word "enthusiasm" comes from the Greek words *En theos* which actually means "in God." God is the source of energy, vitality, and power for those who have come into a relationship with Him through His Son Jesus Christ. We read in Scripture: "He (God) created everything there is—nothing exists that he didn't make" (John 1:3, *TLB*) and "For in him (God) we live and move and have our being" (Acts 17:28).

Commit a New Image of What/Who You Want to Be to God

Through prayer tell God that you want to be a more enthusiastic person. Since enthusiasm is in God, keep plugged into the Creator of life, continually asking Him to mold you into the enthusiastic person you want to

35

become. "Delight yourself in the Lord, and he will give you the desires of your heart" (Ps. 37:4). With God being the source of enthusiasm, there is not a better way to seek enthusiasm than through Him.

There is a special magic with enthusiasm. It has the power to change lives, both yours and those whom you are around. Be challenged to work through these steps towards enthusiasm so you can also possess this unique magic.

Note

1. Peale, Norman Vincent, *Enthusiasm Makes a Difference* (Inglewood Cliffs: Prentice-Hall, 1967), p. 5.

CONFLICT MANAGEMENT

The Tough Road to Better Relationships

My friend Rick Krueger has a favorite saying that goes like this: "Life is tough; and then you die." It might seem that in life we go from tension, to conflict, to trauma. We can expect some conflict and tension in every close, long term relationship that we have. The degree of tension may vary with the circumstances, but the tension is still tension and it's not fun.

Most of us suffer through conflicts because we don't have the knowledge or we don't take the time to deal with tension in relationships when it first arises. Tension begins to grow like mold on stale bread until it overflows and consumes us. Then we may overreact or make irrational decisions or statements that we often regret.

However, many of us would rather eat liver or get a shot at the doctor's rather than deal with the source of our tension. We are the ones who keep everything inside and don't let anyone know how we feel. Neither exploding nor simmering inside is a very effective way of managing tension and conflict. Neither of these methods produces any positive experiences for our relationships.

This chapter is a little different from the others. We will first take a look at some examples of conflict in the Bible and then work through a "conflict cycle" to better understand conflict and how to deal with it.

BIBLICAL CONFLICT

Unresolved Conflicts

When we don't take the time to resolve conflicts we set the stage for very painful experiences—usually for us. When we don't do anything about disagreements, we carry around feelings that bother us. And the person(s) with whom we have the conflict usually knows nothing about the weight we are carrying.

When I was a freshman in high school I had a friend who made up a nickname for me that wasn't very flattering. As a matter of fact it really made me mad when he called me this name. But since my other friends laughed, I pretended that I thought it was funny too. As this name-calling continued I found myself staying away from my friend not because he was a jerk, but because I had a hard time with what he called me.

Our friendship never really grew until I was a senior in high school. At a church retreat I told him that it really bothered me when he called me this name. He had no idea! His response was, "You should have told me; I would have stopped." For almost four years I didn't get close to this person because I was afraid to tell him my feelings. I was experiencing internal pain and he didn't even know it.

Conflict may arise for any number of reasons: jealousy, self-centeredness, possessiveness, personality clashes, and even simple misunderstandings. No matter what the reason for the conflict, it needs to be dealt with in a manner that will save the relationships and enable all of the parties concerned to continue with the process of life. Unresolved conflict has a way of internally affecting us emotionally and spiritually.

Remember, no one is free from conflict, not even the great men in the Bible. Conflict started in the beginning of our history and has since become a part of human relationships (see Gen. 3; 4; 6:13,14; 11:5-9). In the New Testament we see that the apostle Paul and even our Lord Jesus were involved in conflicts.

Jesus' Involvement in Conflicts

It is often hard for us to imagine that Jesus, who has been called the Prince of Peace, was involved in conflicts. But it is true. In Matthew 21:12-17 we read that **Jesus started a conflict** when He entered the Temple and physically threw out those who were buying and selling. At another time in His life He **helped resolve conflict** when He played the peacemaker for a woman who had been caught in adultery (see John 8:3-11). Then there were times when Jesus **avoided conflict** and went His own way (see Luke 4:28-30).

Even Jesus didn't live on this earth without being involved in conflicts and yet He continued to have an effective ministry in spite of all the situations surrounding Him.

Paul and Barnabas' Conflict

In the Bible there is mention of two godly men who couldn't agree with one another on what they should do. Before Paul's second missionary journey he had a conflict with his friend Barnabas (see Acts 15:36-41). These two men were planning on traveling together to preach the Word when they disagreed on who should come along. Barnabas wanted to bring John Mark along and Paul didn't. Paul may have been mad at John Mark because he left them on their last trip. It seems that Barnabas wanted to give John Mark another chance. The Bible says that there was a sharp disagreement between Paul and Barnabas and they went their separate ways (see v. 39). Paul chose Silas to be his companion. Paul and Silas traveled extensively establishing and strengthening churches (see v. 41).

41

It is important to note that there was definitely tension, but Paul and Barnabas dealt with it and continued on with what God had planned for them (encouraging and strengthening churches). This is a great example for us to know about and pattern our actions after.

Conflict Cycle

Once you realize that you will at some time experience conflicts you can look for practical ways to work through them with the least amount of pain and the greatest rewards. Below is a chart of a conflict cycle that can help you to see where you are in a given conflict and where you have to go before you can achieve resolution—your ultimate goal. The cycle looks like this:

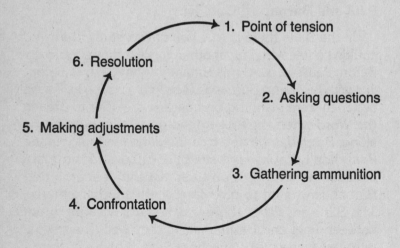

1. Point of tension
2. Asking questions
3. Gathering ammunition
4. Confrontation
5. Making adjustments
6. Resolution

1. Point of Tension

All conflicts have a beginning. This is where you first experience feelings of tension, for whatever reasons, and know that there is some type of friction. At this point your feelings come into play and you feel hurt, betrayed, or misunderstood.

2. Asking Questions

This is the stage when you begin to ask yourself questions. "Is this my fault?" "Do I have the right to be feeling this way?" "What did I do to deserve this?" You are trying to figure out the reasons you feel the way you do. This is the best stage to attempt to resolve your conflict. Ask the questions you've been asking yourself to the other person. It's fine to be naive. In your questioning have the attitude of simply wanting to figure out what is going on. The Bible says not to let the day end with you still being angry (see Eph. 4:26). Right away is often the best time to talk about a conflict.

3. Gathering Ammunition

By the time you get to this stage you are probably upset and have begun to think of ways to put the other person down or of what you can say that will help you get even. Depending on how you manage your conflict, at this point the anger begins to build up to a great explosion. Or you may begin to store your anger away without dealing with it (like I did in the name calling story). This is a dangerous stage and should be avoided when possible!

4. Confrontation

This is a vital stage in the conflict cycle. Confronta-

43

tion means spending time with the other person(s) talking about your conflict. This should be done in a sensitive manner with both sides getting the opportunity to express and explain their feelings. But if there is already too much ammunition gathered, there is a good chance that you will experience a "battle" and defensiveness and separation will join in the war. If confrontation is done in the correct manner the other person can either blow the relationship off and forget about the existing relationship or agree to change and make adjustments. Obviously, the latter is preferred.

5. Making Adjustments

If the confrontation went well, there is need to make adjustments so that the relationship can improve. Both parties need to agree on the changes. Expectations need to be discussed. You may find that it will be more beneficial for both of you to do some of the changing so that you are a team in bringing resolution to the conflict. Cathy and I love this stage; it is the "making up" stage where we both make a commitment to one another to be better or try harder.

6. Resolution

This is when the conflict is finally over and almost everything is back to normal. You need to realize that you may still have painful feelings caused by the conflict, especially if you were hurt. It's okay to still have these feelings but it is important to let the other person(s) know that you are forgiving.

Conflict is painful! Confrontation can be even more painful. But it must be done. Confrontation is vital to change and change is vital to the resolution of the conflict. We all know that if we have a pulse and are still breathing we are going to experience conflict. It's difficult but it's a part of experiencing relationships with other people. God has made many experiences— painful but also joyful—available to us through our relationships with others.

COMPETITION

Do You Always Have to Win?

As we watch professional athletes we view them giving their all to be the best and to win. For them winning is everything! The better they play and the more they win the better their prospects when they negotiate their next contract. Basically it comes down to this: the better they play the more money they will make. Those of us who aren't professional athletes don't have this type of performance pressure . . . or we shouldn't. But whether we play the piano, paint, or play on the basketball team, we are still competing. Actually, we are always competing! We compete against ourselves, against a standard, and against others.

Just this morning I was wondering if this chapter would be helpful for other people. Then at 3:00 this afternoon my church high school group got together to play street hockey and just about killed each other. I broke up at least three fights and took stick whips into my shins until I could barely walk. We had one argument about whether one of the goals was a clean goal or a ricochet. Why argue? It was still a goal.

The statement of the day came when one of the students said, "We are not going to quit until we win!"

After the game I hobbled back to my office and was convinced. This definitely is a needed chapter.

In this chapter we will take a look at a few attitudes that can be dangerous to a Christian's growth and witness if not handled properly. Then we will look at some realistic ways in which everyone (competitive or not) can develop some positive attitudes that will help them in their pursuit of not becoming a goon.

COMPETITIVE ATTITUDES

Do Anything to Win Attitude

There are some people that place such a big emphasis on winning that they will do whatever it may take to win; even if it is going to hurt others. Some of you may remember the 1980 Boston marathon where Rosie Ruiz crossed the finish line in a world record time only to be later disqualified because she didn't run the entire race. She had jumped into the pack of runners near the end of the 26-mile run. Rosie was not only disqualified she also stole the show of the real female winner. The Bible says, "An athlete is not crowned unless he competes according to the rules" (2 Tim. 2:5, *RSV*).

Years ago, a soap box derby champion was disqualified because he used a specially designed, illegal magnet to help him get down the hill faster. Why? To win of course. Some people sacrifice their integrity for the short-lived pleasure of winning.

We need to see and help others understand that winning isn't everything. The old cliche that goes, "Winning isn't everything, it's how you play the game" seems outdated because there are too many people and teams that will do anything to win. Even young children are pressured by their parents to win.

When my younger sister, Stacy, was ten years old she decided to try to play soccer for the first time. She was placed in a league filled with girls eleven to thirteen and turned out to be the only girl on the team who had never played before. She didn't get to play very much. When

50

she did play the coach hid her in a position of little action. During an important and close game it was time for Stacy to play and she heard one of the parents say, "Now that she is going to play we will lose for sure."

Nervously Stacy bumbled into the game, ears ringing with the spiteful words. Stacy's team did lose the game because that parent's thoughtless comment made her fall apart. Yet she felt as if it was her fault and didn't even want to finish the season. Stacy did not play soccer the next season because of a painful experience motivated out of a parent's great desire to win.

Winning shouldn't be so important that you compromise your integrity. Sure it's fun to win but to make winning a supreme goal can be destructive to your personality. You will also set yourself up for failure because you can't win at everything. As difficult as that may be for you to understand it will be to your advantage to realize now that you can't win at everything in life.

I stress the importance of not comparing our accomplishments to those of others in my book *Creative Dating*. I think it is important to develop this habit of not comparing because if you look far enough someone will always be able to talk better, outperform, look better, or in some other way outdo you.

I Hate to Lose Attitude

People who will do anything to win usually have a hard time losing. Their competitive nature is so intense that they drive themselves towards winning and when they lose (and they do) they hate it.

Recently, our high school group had a football game in which one high school Bible study group challenged another. It was a wild game! Each group wanted to win so badly that they brought in varsity football players from their schools to help. (It turned out to be a great tool for outreach.)

After the game was over we were walking off the field and one of the students said to me, "I hate to lose."

I quickly responded by saying, "We didn't lose we tied."

He then said, "I was always taught if you tied you might as well consider it a loss."

How unfortunate! By placing so much emphasis on winning, a fun, evenly matched game was not even enjoyed. It would have been better to walk away thinking, "Hey that was a tough fun game."

Those who hate to lose are usually the same ones who are considered poor sports and who do the most judging and complaining. I played organized, competitive sports for twelve years. I realize it is fun to win, especially when there is something at stake. But to take competition so seriously that you are very bothered by losing can be destructive to both your personality and your relationships.

Evaluating Your Self Worth Based on Your Performance

If your self-image is based on whether you win or lose, you will probably find yourself being incredibly competitive. When I was in high school I was the most competitive person that you could ever meet. I would do anything to win, and I did. When I lost I wasn't fun to be around. Basically when it came to competition I was a goon.

Then one Sunday night my youth group was playing "ultimate frisbee" in the church parking lot. I was being my usual competitive self, knocking people around and doing whatever it would take to win when my leader, Jim Burns, pulled me aside.

Jim said, "Doug, you are a good athlete but you will never be an effective minister for Jesus Christ if you continue to act the way you do during competition."

That night I went home and reflected on what Jim had said. I realized that one of the reasons I wanted to win so badly was that winning was good for my ego. It feels good to be on the winning side. It's nice to be chosen to play on the winning team. It feels good to receive compliments for playing well. These are all selfish reasons for wanting to win. I knew I had to change.

You may find this reflected in your friends. The people who are the most competitive may have the lowest self-images.

Years later I now understand what Jim was trying to tell me. By focusing on myself, trying so hard to be a winner I was more interested in me than I was in the well-being and the success of others. To be an effective minister of Jesus Christ (which is what Christians are called to be) we must learn to take our eyes off of ourselves and focus them on the Lord and on others.

HAVING THE PROPER ATTITUDE OF COMPETITION

Develop an Attitude of Fun

Learning to have fun while competing has nothing to do with talent. You can be unathletic, musically goofy, and academically stupid and you can still learn to have a winning attitude. A winning attitude is one that views life as fun. It is an expression of thankfulness for the talents and abilities that God has given you.

I love the bumper sticker that reads ARE WE HAVING FUN YET? You may be losing a football game by 100 points and still be having fun. You may have come in fifth place in a speech contest and still have had fun because of the people you met and the opportunity you had to share your speech. If you can remember that winning doesn't always equate with fun you will come out ahead.

One winning attitude can turn around an entire team. Continually remind yourself, your friends, and your team that you are having a good time. Life can be fun and should be lived as though we are acknowledging all the great things that God put on this earth. My friend Todd Temple has taught me to think of this earth as a huge playground that God has created for us to live on and enjoy as we worship and serve Him.

Focus on Doing Your Best

When you are competing, do your best. God has given you talents. Use them. Develop an attitude of wanting to do the very best you can. The apostle Paul told the church in Corinth, "Whether you eat or drink or whatever you do, do it to the glory of God" (1 Cor. 10:31). Giving it your very best can be a way of giving glory to God for what He has given you. Obviously doing your best to the glory of God does not involve an overly competitive attitude, hurting others, or drawing attention to yourself.

You will often hear Christian performers being interviewed after a great performance say that it wasn't them that performed but it was God. This has always struck me as funny. I've always wanted to say to a Christian musician, "I could have sworn that was you and not God because I saw your mouth move when you sang." What they should say is that God has given them the power and the abilities to perform. It was their performance but it was God who graciously gave them the ability to do what they did. Do what you do to the best of your God-given ability and do everything to the glory of God.

> And whatever you do, whether in word or deed, do it all in the name of the Lord Jesus, giving thanks to God the Father through him. (Col. 3:17)

Realize That God's Acceptance Is for Winners *and* Losers

It is very important to understand that God loves you not for what you do nor how good you are but for simply being His creation. God loves us so much that He gave His only son to die for us so that we might live eternally if we believe in Him (see John 3:16).

It's really hard to understand why God loves us so much even though we are sinners and disobedient to Him. But the important and saving fact is that He does.

> God demonstrates his own love for us in this: While we were still sinners, Christ died for us. (Rom. 5:8)

We may be the last pick on every team that we ever try out for, but we are Number One to God. God doesn't treat us any differently, if we lose the big game or make a mistake on our solo performance. And He doesn't reward us any differently if we spend the rest of our competitive years on a losing team. He will still pick us for His All-Star Team.

If we really understand this then we can do our very best for God and not be so concerned about having destructively competitive attitudes. We can begin to enjoy losing as much as winning just because we know that God has us on His team.

GIVING

The Percentage Game

In the world in which we have the privilege of living there is a massive appeal for us to become takers. We are encouraged to take whatever we can get our hands on. We live in a self-centered society that tells us to look out for Number One and that Number One is ourselves. Even Christians are not free from this selfish attitude.

Recently I was at a Christian convention where a professional musician gave a concert to approximately 1,500 people. In the middle of her set she mentioned that her record company was giving away 100 free records to the first people who arrived at the company's booth *after* the concert. Immediately, there was a rush of people racing to the booth wanting her album right away. These people were more concerned about getting a free album than they were about being rude to the performer.

This selfish attitude is in complete opposition to what God desires for us. God desires for us to be givers, not takers. God wants us to give 100 percent in some areas of our lives and smaller portions in other areas. But the important point is that we are called to give.

GOD WANTS 100 PERCENT OF . . .

Your Life, Relationships, and Material Possessions

The Bible tells us that if we are to follow Jesus then we need to love Him more than we love anything or anyone else (see Luke 14:26). The apostle Paul tells us that we are to present our bodies as a living sacrifice to God (see Rom. 12:1). As you can see these verses do not indicate that God wants a portion but that He wants everything, our entire lives.

In the Old Testament God asked Abraham to sacrificially murder his only son, Isaac, whom he loved very much. God was testing Abraham's commitment to Him. When God saw that Abraham was actually going to go through with the sacrifice He spared Isaac's life and blessed Abraham for his faith and obedience (see Gen. 22).

God wants us to have faith like Abraham had. When we put other things before our relationship with God, our Christianity is out of balance. Perfect balance is when we give 100 percent of our lives to God so that He can use us the way He wants us to be used. He is a jealous God when it comes to having other things before Him (see Exod. 20:5). That is why it was so important for Abraham to be tested. God desired to use Abraham and wanted to make sure that he was faithful. Because of Abraham's faith God used him to become the pioneer of our faith.

Many Christians claim that God is the most important thing in their lives and yet when it comes down to it they usually give more time and attention to their material possessions and relationships with other people. I know of many people who are more excited about their car or the thought of owning a better car than they are about their God. Love for their car has become their "Isaac" (that thing which they love more dearly than anything else). My "Isaac" is in my commitment to human relationships. I often find myself putting my relationship with Cathy and other friends before my relationship with God. This is wrong!

We need to sacrifice our "Isaac"(s) on the altar of faith and prove to God that He is Number One in our lives. God chose to bless Abraham when He saw his faith and obedience were greater than his love for his only son Isaac. A question that we need to ask ourselves is "are my possessions and relationships so important to me that I am willing to miss out on blessings from God?"

God wants us to have the faith and obedience of Abraham. He wants us to give up our Isaacs, those things that we love more dearly than anything else, and make Him Number One in our lives. That is giving 100 percent!

While it is important to realize that God wants 100 percent in the areas of faith and obedience, there are other areas where He asks for a smaller percentage. He knows that we are capable of giving 100 percent of our lives, relationships, and material possessions, but in the following two areas God seems to settle for a little less. In no way does this mean that God doesn't feel these areas are important. It just shows that a smaller percentage is sufficient to illustrate our obedience to Him.

In a broad sense these two areas are interrelated with our life and material possessions of which we are to give 100 percent to God. But in a more defined sense, these specific acts of giving are demonstrations of our 100 percent faith in God.

GOD WANTS A PERCENTAGE OF . . .

Your Time

There is a principle in the Old Testament called the Sabbath. (We will look at this in greater depth in the

61

Reflection chapter.) The Sabbath is a special time the people set aside for God. The observance of the Sabbath was carried into the New Testament and today there are still people who religiously observe it.

This Sabbath time was given to God in worship and in acknowledgement of His greatness. How much time do you give to God? How much personal time? How much time do you volunteer to the church for God? God doesn't ask for 100 percent of our time, but He does ask that we give Him a percentage of it. Are you giving one-seventh of your time to God?

Your Money

In the Old Testament people were required by law to give a portion (tithe) of their money. When all of the requirements were added up, they had to give over 20 percent of their income. In the New Testament we find that we are no longer under the law and required to give. But under the new covenant of Christ we are to give as we prosper.

Christ got upset with the Pharisees who seemed to be more concerned about being legalistic about their giving than they were with showing love for God (see Matt. 23:23). Christ is more concerned about the attitude of the heart when we give than He is in the amount we give. Here is a beautiful illustration of this point:

Jesus sat down opposite the place where the offerings were put and watched the crowd putting their money into the temple treasury. Many rich people threw in large amounts. But a poor widow came and put in two very small coins, worth only a fraction of a penny. Calling his disciples to him, Jesus said, "I tell you the truth, this poor widow has put more into the treasury than all the others. They all gave out of their wealth; but she, out of her poverty, put in everything—all she had to live on. (Mark 12:41-44)

Giving should demonstrate our obedience to God. Because we love Him and have given 100 percent of ourselves to Him we feel the need and desire to give some of our money back to Him so that His ministry might continue.

Remember, God is concerned with the attitude of your heart. If you don't want to give, God will know it and there will be no reward for you. The Bible says, "Everyone must make up his own mind as to how much he should give. Don't force anyone to give more than he really wants to, for cheerful givers are the ones God prizes" (2 Cor. 9:7, *TLB*).

Whether you give 10 percent or 50 percent the point is that you give with a cheerful heart like the poor widow who gave knowing that God would honor her and take care of her. If God honors cheerful givers then our challenge should be to become hilarious givers.

HOW DO YOU BECOME A GIVER?

Begin Biblically
We have already seen that God desires for us to give, not because we need to nor because we want to receive God's blessings, but because we are obedient to God

63

and giving is a response of our love for Him. We are also told that we are to give with a cheerful heart. Jesus also gives us another instruction for giving and that is to give without bringing attention to yourself when you give. One of the students in my youth group told me that he gives an offering of 10 dollars a week. He wanted a positive response from me. This is a wrong attitude! Giving is between you and God. Jesus tried to explain this in the Sermon on the Mount by telling people not to sound trumpets when they give but to give in secret (see Matt. 6:1-4). Jesus said, "Your Father who sees what is done in secret will reward you" (Matt. 6:4).

Giving in secret is difficult because most of us want others to know how good we are or how righteous we are. But this defeats the purpose of giving! If we try to bring attention to ourselves then God knows our hearts are not right. I don't know about you but I would rather receive my rewards from God than from the few people who may see me give.

Find a Real Life Example

Finding an example could help you understand any of the qualities discussed in this book. But it particularly helps to find someone who you recognize as being a giving person. Then, try to model yourself after him or her. By finding someone like this the quality can be seen as attainable.

When it comes to giving I watch my friend Alan Smith. He is the most generous, selfless man I know. He is always looking for ways to give. His life-style has become a challenge to those of us who spend time with him. Alan doesn't give to bring glory to himself but gives because he loves God and wants to bring honor to Him.

His daily prayer is: "Lord, show me how I can give of myself today to someone who needs your love." Accept the challenge to find an Alan Smith, a person you can watch and learn from. If you look hard enough you'll find someone like him.

Give Anonymously, Generously, Voluntarily, and Personally

In his book, *Improving Your Serve,* Chuck Swindoll points out four ways in which we are to give.

Anonymously: This is a great test of selfless giving. Those who possess a true giver's heart are embarrassed when their name is mentioned with their giving.

Generously: Giving liberally of your time, yourself, and your money communicates both a faith in God's provisions and an excitement for giving away the blessing God has given you.

Voluntarily: We have already mentioned the fact, that giving needs to be done cheerfully, not because of arm-twisting.

Personally: It is important that we be personally involved in our giving. When Cathy and I give to an organization, we pray for them and offer ourselves to them in whatever ways we can. This helps us to know where our money is going as well as it shows the organization that we are truly behind them.

This point cannot be overemphasized: giving is our response to our love and obedience to God. May your faith and your giving outgrow your dreams as you cheerfully become the giver that God desires for you to be.

TRANSPARENCY

An Open Window to Better Relationships

Even if we are not goons most of us still run around in constant fear; fear that we won't be accepted for who we are; fear that we will be laughed at; and fear that we will be rejected. The result of this fear is seen in our lives when we put on false masks and try to become someone we really aren't. We hide behind these security masks as if they were shields. When we enter the "battle" of relationships we put our shields up so we won't get hurt.

While this is happening, another side of us has a deep inner craving to tell someone who we really are and what we really are like without our shields. But this is not easy to do. Just when we begin to be real we get afraid and hide behind our shields of protection where it is safe and comfortable.

Being transparent means opening up to another person and letting him or her know who you *really* are. It is a tough task to attempt! Most of us would rather settle for the easy route of being a goon than risk being rejected. In this chapter we will look at the benefits of being transparent as well as some practical ways in which we can accomplish this goal.

BENEFITS OF BEING TRANSPARENT

Transparency Strengthens Your Friendships

Being transparent will strengthen your friendships because you are letting someone else know you in an

69

intimate way. By sharing dreams, fantasies, struggles, fears, and doubts with another person you will develop a sense of bonding two different hearts into a closer union.

When I was a junior in high school I thought Jeff Genoway was my best friend because we did things together, laughed, talked about girls, and basically enjoyed each other's company. Our relationship changed one Friday night, on the way to a high school football game, when I risked being rejected and ask Jeff a personal question about sexuality that I didn't understand. Jeff didn't treat me like I was stupid for not knowing. We openly discussed my question. After that evening Jeff and I began to talk about everything. We grew closer than we ever were before because we had begun to rid ourselves of our shields and share with each other what we were *really* like. This turned out to be one of my most rewarding relationships. To this day Jeff and I share anything and everything. I know that no matter what I say or do Jeff will still care about and accept me.

Transparency Helps Other People

There are times when many of us feel that we are the only people in the world struggling with a certain problem or having a certain horrible thought. We tend to die in a pile of guilt or feel overly sorry for ourselves. By being transparent we learn that other people have many of the same problems or thoughts as we do. This brings great relief! We don't rejoice that other people have problems, but we do rejoice because we know that we aren't alone.

Transparency has changed my life! Right after I became a Christian I began to hang around with my

70

youth minister so I could learn more about Christianity. The more time I spent with this godly man the more I felt like I couldn't be a Christian because I wasn't perfect; he didn't seem to have any problems or hurts. I was going through all of my weekly problems wondering why I was still struggling so much. I thought Christianity was perfectionism and I was ready to give it up because I was convinced I couldn't become perfect.

At about this same time, a counselor from the church, Mike Driggs, moved into my family's home. I really respected Mike and enjoyed having him live with us. Within a month of Mike's arrival his long-term girl-friend broke up with him, he had a major knee operation that put him on crutches for months, and he had family problems. Mike told me about these struggles and the hurt and pain that accompanied them. I lived with Mike as he cried out his questions and threw his crutches in disbelief and anger. Yet I saw that Mike continued to love and follow God. Mike's transparency showed me that Christianity wasn't perfectionism. I decided to stick it out.

Mike's tranparency helped me and changed my life. Being transparent is now a characteristic of my ministry because I know that it helps others realize that they are not alone.

Transparency Helps Us

In a transparent relationship, there will be times when you need to have the other person listen to all the struggles you are going through. There might even be times when you list all your sins and ask your friend to help you be accountable for being a stronger Christian. In the book of James there is an appeal for us to "con-

71

fess your sins to each other and pray for each other so that you may be healed" (Jas. 5:16). Transparency gives us the freedom to list our weaknesses before another person. Notice that James says, "so that you may be healed." There is a real healing process that takes place when we confess to someone else areas in our lives that need help. The act of confession to another person (in addition to God who forgives us) helps us get these feelings out in the open where they can be seen in a different light and a new perspective. In addition, this accountability gives us greater reason to take action in resolving our sins.

HOW TO BECOME MORE TRANSPARENT

Be Selective

To start off with, choose one friend who you feel you can trust. It would be an unwise move for you to try to let everyone in your group know your *real* self all at once. Everyone may not care and you may experience the rejection that you fear. One person is easier to communicate with and if you know they care about you then you are ready to go. This does not mean that you want to give up your other friendships; simply select one person with whom you can learn to become more transparent.

Begin Slowly

A good rule to follow in this practice of becoming more transparent is to start slowly. Begin slowly and evaluate the reaction of the other person. Does he or she care about you? Will he or she tell this to someone else? Can you trust this person? You may find that if you get hurt in your attempt to become more transparent you will respond much more slowly, if at all, in your next attempt.

Challenge for the Same Transparency

The healthiest transparent relationships are the ones in which both people are letting their shields down. If you find that the other person is doing all the listening, you may need to challenge him or her to slowly become more transparent with you. I am much more willing to risk letting another person know me better if that other person is also risking.

Be a Good Partner

Being a good partner in transparency is very important. Here are four solid rules to keep in mind when you are on the receiving end:

1. *Don't give advice*—Sit on your opinion and your advice and simply listen. Too often we want to spout off our brilliant wisdom without listening. What the other person needs is an active listener. (See more detailed section on listening in the Nonverbal Communication chapter.)
2. *Don't act shocked*—When someone reveals an intimate dream, fantasy, or thought don't act like you can't believe they would ever think of such a thing. Simply accept and appreciate what they have to say before you respond.
3. *Don't judge*—This is so easy to do! Jesus tells us to remove the log out of our own eye before we look at the speck in our brother's eye (see Matt. 7:1-5). If someone experiences judgment then they will be afraid of not being accepted and that will bring them

73

back to their initial fear and their transparency will be quenched.

4. *Don't abuse confidence*—You are a true goon if you go out and tell someone what was shared with you in a transparent and trusting manner. This is the easiest way to lose the special gift of having someone with whom you can be transparent.

God wants to bless us so that we might enjoy Him and this earthly playground that He gave us. Yet we so often find ways to take advantage of His blessings and mess things up. God gave us one another so that we might share with each other in an intimate and beautiful manner. Being transparent with someone can prove to be one of the most rewarding experiences we can have because of the wonderful feeling that comes when we openly give ourselves to another person and they accept us and give themselves back.

God loves us not for what we do but for who we are. My prayer is that you would find someone in your life who reflects this godly attitude; it will change your life.

AFFIRMATION

The Life-Changing Power of Words

You probably have heard the saying, "Sticks and stones will break my bones but words will never hurt me." This is a gross lie! Words are very powerful, especially when they are directed at someone! Words have the ability to change lives for the better or destroy them. Each of us holds the key to unlocking tremendous power through words that shoot from our mouths every day. The Bible says that the tongue is a small thing but it can do great damage as well as bring joy (see Jas. 3:5).

The people around us are dying to hear positive words. We all crave and need positive strokes to keep us going. Yet the majority of what we hear is negative. "Sit down!" "Shut up!" "Leave me alone!" "Can't you do anything right?" "Is that your face or did your neck throw up?" "Why didn't you get that in on time?" These are just a few negative phrases that are constantly spoken. We would much rather hear: "Hey you look great today!" "You did a really good job on this!" "It's good to see you today!" "I really liked what you had to say in class today; I can tell you are a thinker." Positive words have a way of making us feel warm inside while negative words seem to freeze our insides with an uncomfortable and painful feeling.

When we constantly hear negative input we begin to believe it. If people repeatedly tell you that you are ugly, you will probably begin to act and feel ugly. Bill Glass in his book, *Expect to Win,* says that of the thousands of prisoners he has talked with, 90 percent of them say,

77

"My dad always told me I'd end up behind bars, and I didn't let him down."[1] These inmates lived out the negative words that they heard. This truth is tragic. Yet it can bring us great joy to know that what we say to people has the power to affect their lives in a positive way.

This chapter is written so that we might better understand the incredible force that our affirming words can have on others and how we can better use this life-changing quality.

RESULTS OF AFFIRMATION

Others Feel Good About Themselves

Compliments are one form of affirmation. When we receive a compliment we feel good and think to ourselves, "Hey somebody noticed something good about me!" We feel as if someone cares enough not only to notice something nice, but also to mention it. This helps us feel good about ourselves.

God wants His people to feel special. We are special! We were each uniquely created by God while we were still in our mothers' wombs (Ps. 139). We were special enough for God to create this world and to send his Son to die for us. Make it your goal to help others feel the specialness that God can offer. You will feel great in return as you see their eyes light up in surprise and thankfulness. Mark Twain once said that he could live two months on one good compliment; and so can your friends.

Builds Confidence

Affirmation can be a strong force in building confidence. If someone affirms an ability you have, you will be more willing to put it to use. If you are constantly told that you are no good, you will be programmed to fail. (Remember the prisoners?)

Four of the most important words in the English language are *I believe in you.* My father and my friend Jim Burns are two people who have constantly told me this. When I was struggling to get through high school, college, and graduate school, they would tell me "I believe in you."

Knowing that someone believes in you makes a world of difference. Every time I hear these words I am reminded of the positive support I received when I participated in sports and my parents cheered for me from the sidelines. I felt as though I could do anything because people were on my side and believed in me.

There are many people in your life who believe in you but until they verbalize it you may feel that you are all alone. Who do you believe in but haven't actually told? They may be holding back in fear. The words they need to build their confidence are "I believe in you." Try saying these words and watch the results.

Brings Out the Best in People

I coach soccer with my pastor Tim Timmons. A few years ago we were coaching a team of six- and seven-year-olds. At our first practice we knew that we didn't have a great team and there was little chance that we would get into the play-offs. So we decided that we would constantly affirm our players so they would at least feel good about themselves when they lost. They heard positive words for not only their performance but for who they were as people. By the time the season started we had fifteen kids who thought they were just

79

the greatest. And that's what they became. We never lost a game! To our surprise we found that by affirming them, their hidden talents came out and they played their very best. This is no coaching secret, it's common sense.

When people feel better about themselves they will look smarter, play harder, and do better. One of the major points in Dale Carnegie's best-selling book, *How to Win Friends and Influence People,* is that people respond to their greatest potential when they feel good about themselves.

Changes Lives

Jesus changed the life of a big mouth fisherman when he changed Simon's name to Peter (John 1:42). Jesus saw past all of Simon's sins and attitude problems and named him, much to the surprise of Simon's friends, *Peter,* which means rock. In the book of Acts we see that the very foundation of the early church was built on this rock. Jesus changed Peter's life by simply affirming him through a name change.

The 1980 Miss America was Cheryl Prewitt. I heard her say that when she was only four or five years old, she hung around her father's small, country grocery store. Almost daily the milkman would come, and she would follow him to watch as he lined the display cases with shiny bottles of milk. He always greeted her with, "How's my little Miss America?" At first she giggled, but she soon became comfortable with it. Before long, it was a childhood fantasy, then a teenage dream, and finally, a solid goal. It all started with a word spoken daily to a young, impressionable mind. It became imbedded in the subconscious. It became a prayer and a reality. Who was responsible: the milkman, the subconscious of a growing child, or God? I'd say all three, but lean toward God, because He created them all.[2]

As you can see, the power is so strong that even lives can be changed by the utterance of affirming words. Realize the power and affirm wisely.

STEPS TOWARD AFFIRMATION

Realize that Affirming Others Doesn't Make You Look Bad

One of the major reasons that we fail to affirm others is because of our own low self-images. We are afraid that if we build someone else up, we will make ourselves look bad. We don't want others to think that they are better than ourselves. Or when we choose to affirm, we will do it in private so that others won't think the person we are complimenting is better than we are. This is a selfish attitude. We deprive others of love and positive words because we are afraid that they will look better than ourselves. The Bible tells us, "Love one another with brotherly affection; outdo one another in showing honor" (Rom. 12:10, *RSV*). This is difficult to do but if we can get to where we want others to look good regardless of how we look in comparison, we are on our way to having a ministry of affirmation. Read carefully these words that illustrate the importance of loving others.

81

Most of us know our need to be loved and try to seek the love that we need from others . . . if we seek the love which we need, we will never find it . . . we must face the fact that to be loved, we must become lovable . . . . If a person, however, seeks not to receive love, but rather to give it, he will become lovable and he will most certainly be loved in the end.[3]

Search for the Positive

If you actively search you will see that it is easy to find some quality or feature that is worthy of affirmation in every person. The key to positive affirmation is that you are sincere in what you say. Others will sense if you are insincere in your affirmation. In that case it is probably better to not say anything until you can speak with integrity and sincerity. You wouldn't want to say, "You played a great game!" if the person you are trying to affirm struck out three times and committed four errors. (This would be a good time for comfort rather than compliments.)

Also in your search for the positive make sure that what you think is affirming is actually affirming to the recipient. For example you wouldn't say, "It's really nice that you don't sweat much for a fat person" or "Your hair looks great. It is usually greasy." Search for the truly positive.

Affirm Continually

Constantly be affirming to those with whom you come in contact. Place reminders on your steering wheel, mirror, locker, and shoes that tell you to keep affirming. Make affirmation a habit. It can be one of the most positive habits that you will ever have in your life. Soon you will be known as the person who makes others feel special about themselves.

Use Your Affirmation as a Witness of God's Love

Affirming can be a tremendous ministry. This ministry will have far greater implications than just making others feel better about themselves. You can actually begin to reveal to others the beautiful love God has placed in your heart.

Jesus tells us that the contents of our heart will influence what we have to say. "For a man's heart determines his speech. A good man's speech reveals the rich treasures within him" (Matt. 12:34-35, *TLB*). Your positive words will begin to reflect the radiance of God's love that was given to you when you came into a relationship with Him. You can also use this as a guide to where your heart is. Do positive or negative words come out of your mouth? Your heart trouble may show up in your speech. This beautiful sentence says it all: "There is no human being who will not eventually respond to love if only he can realize that he is loved."[4]

Pray that God may use your affirming words to reflect the source of where your affirmation originates. It is from God Himself.

Notes

1. Bill Glass, *Expect to Win* (Waco: Word Books, 1981), p. 35.
2. Glass, *Expect to Win*, p. 34.
3. John Powell, *Why Am I Afraid to Love?* (Allen: Argus Communications, 1967), pp. 104, 105.
4. Powell, *Why Am I Afraid to Love?*, p. 12.

NONVERBAL COMMUNICATION

What You Don't Say Speaks Loudly

When I was in junior high I would come home from school and as soon as I walked in the door I would shout "I'm home." I would then go quickly to the refrigerator to grab something to eat, move downstairs, and plant my body in front of the television until baseball practice. Before long my mom would make her way into the room and ask me the same question every mother asks when you get home from school, "How was your day dear?" I would always reply, "Fine" with little or no emotion. Then she would persist and ask, "Well, what did you do today?" and I would give her the familiar answer. "Nothing" I'd say as I continued to stare at my favorite repeat TV show. My mom would then let out a deep breath, roll her eyes back, and say, "It's always good to talk with you Doug" with a brilliant sarcastic tone that only my mom could get away with.

One day, on the way home from school, I remembered something my friend had told me he did and I decided to give it a try. I was going to give my mom her wish and tell her what I had done at school—*exactly* what I had done! When she asked me her daily question I told her everything starting with the moment I arrived at school. "Well mom when I got to school, got off my bike, and undid my combination lock 15-23-8 and locked up my bike to Rick Krueger's bike. Then we both walked to my locker and I waved to Patty Daum who was walking with Pam Sears; they are so cute! Then we went to Mr. Owen's P.E. class. But I didn't dress out because

Todd Dean tried to light my shorts on fire. He's such a pyro." I'm sure you get the picture. I did this with my mom for three straight days and, for some reason, on the fourth day my mom didn't ask me her famous questions anymore. I had talked her ear off, my friend's idea worked.

As I look over this daily scene I see that my mom and I communicated several times. First of all, I verbally communicated that I was home when I came yelling through the door, then I communicated that I was hungry when I took food from the refrigerator and expressed my boredom by slouching in front of the television. My mom not only verbally communicated a question but also communicated a concern for me as a person. Because of my non-enthusiastic response I communicated a message that television was so important that I wasn't interested in talking with my mom. In her second question Mom communicated that she *really* did want to talk to me. But finally she gave up and in her departing sarcastic response communicated her frustration for our lack of communication.

As you can see we communicate in a variety of ways and are capable of sending messages that we may not really want to give at all. Communication is a very complicated skill. Communication specialists point out that there are actually six messages that can come through when we communicate.

1. What you mean to say.

2. What you actually say.

3. What the other person hears.

4. What the other person thinks he hears.

5. What the other person says about what you said.

6. What you think the other person said about what you said.

Sounds confusing, doesn't it? It is and yet communication is very important to who we are and what we are able to do as servants of Christ. It is vital that we learn how to communicate so we can effectively share the message of salvation in Christ.

Yet the type of communication mentioned in this chapter is called nonverbal communication. (This does not mean that verbal communication is not important.) Defined simply as communication without the use of words, reports show that communication is only 7 percent verbal (words only), 38 percent vocal (tones and inflections), and 55 percent facial (nonverbal). This doesn't mean that words are meaningless in communication; they just aren't as vital as we may believe.

The Bible has much to say about the power of words and stresses the importance of controlling the tongue. But the truth is that what we do nonverbally speaks louder than what we say. Jesus tells His disciples this when He tells them, "Love one another. By this all men will know that you are my disciples, if you love one another" (John 13:34,35). Isn't it true that it is easier to feel love than to hear about love?

In this chapter I want to briefly mention two vital ways in which we miss the mark in our attempt to communicate. Then, I will present three ways in which we can better understand and apply positive nonverbal communication in our own lives.

MISSING THE MARK IN COMMUNICATION

Listening but Not Listening

When I was in college one of my instructors told me that for about half (50 percent) of our day we listen, we hear half of what is said, we understand half of that, we believe half of that, and finally we remember half of what we believe. I write all this to say that even though we spend a great deal of our time listening we really don't hear what is being said. And if we are not hearing what is being said then we are not receiving communication. Listening is a very important part of nonverbal communication. When we show that we are not listening we communicate a message that the other person isn't important to us.

Recently I was at a convention where I was approached by a man who asked me a question about my church. As I began to answer his question I saw that he was looking right past me nodding his head in an attempt to appear like he was paying attention. For all I know he may have heard every word I said but without looking at me I felt (and feelings are very important in communication) like he wasn't hearing me. It is awkward and embarrassing to feel like you are standing in a crowd talking to yourself.

What do you nonverbally communicate to your family and friends when they are talking? Do they feel like you are genuinely interested in what they are saying? Are you? You should be if you value other people. Can you imagine Jesus, if He were here talking with us today, looking past us or giving us the impression that He isn't interested? Don't you think Jesus would be waiting for every word we might have to say because He cares so deeply about you and me? Just like Jesus, we communicate that we care when we actively listen.

Jumping to Conclusions

In all forms of communication we have to interpret what we think the other person is trying to say. In non-verbal communication this is difficult because, in some ways, we have to read the other person's mind because we can't hear what they are thinking.

The other night I was writing, and was in one of my intense gazes, when Cathy came home. I looked up over the computer and she said I had a look on my face that nonverbally communicated, "You told me you were going to be home at 6:30 and now it's 7:00; where have you been?" Since I had not said a word she jumped to the conclusion that I was mad and went into the kitchen without making a sound. When I came out of my intense stare I wondered why Cathy didn't say anything to me and quickly jumped to the conclusion that she was disappointed with me since I had forgotten to take the meat out of the freezer. When we finally sat and talked we realized that we perceived each other in a wrong manner.

This misunderstanding in communication happens all the time. Think about it. Someone gives us a dirty look and we think they hate us when, in actuality, their underwear may be too tight and is causing them to look that way. Or how about when we pull up to a person in the other car and he or she smiles at us and we think they like us but they are really laughing at our looks. It is so easy to jump to conclusions when we don't take the time to accurately attempt to interpret nonverbal communication. This puts us in a position to be wrong and/ or to get ourselves in trouble.

HITTING THE TARGET IN COMMUNICATION

Eye Contact

This is an easy concept to understand since our eyes are such an active part of our communication process. If your eyes are actively looking at the person you are communicating with, you will make them feel that you are interested in what they are saying. Eye contact also communicates that they are special enough for you to be listening to them.

Some people have a hard time looking others in the eye. I used to have this problem. I overcame it by finding someone who is really good at making eye contact and studying him. I watched my friend Todd Alexander and the way he "talks" with his eyes. He makes me feel very comfortable because his expressive eyes show that he is concerned and interested in what I have to say. Todd makes me feel accepted, and that encourages me to be open and honest in our relationship. The response he receives is amazing because his eyes communicate concern. All I can say is that practice makes perfect; so keep trying.

Body Language

Most of us are unaware of our own body language and how it communicates. But the fact is, we often communicate different feelings and attitudes which are interpreted in a variety of ways by other people.

If you and I were to get together and you wanted to tell me some of your problems or just wanted to talk it would be important for me to remember not only to look at you, but also to pay attention to you with the way I positioned my body. If you had something important to talk about, I would be rude to slouch in my chair turned away from you. Right?

I had the privilege of helping teach a youth ministry class at a nearby college. There I met a student who gave me this look that I interpreted as, "What do you think you know to be teaching in this class?" Now that was intimidating! Another girl slouched so much in her seat that I could barely see her face. Half the time she slept in class. Talk about nonverbal communication! She didn't want to be in the class and she wasn't afraid of letting anybody know it!

Let your body language communicate that you want to be there and are, again, interested in the person with whom you are communicating.

Touching

Touch is a very important physical aspect of our lives. God created us as physical creatures. From the very moment we came from our mothers' wombs we required and desired touch and affection. As we grow we still need that same touch and caring. Touch is a form of communication. It communicates love; it calms our fears; it makes us feel comfortable; and it especially makes us feel wanted and special. If you can master when it is appropriate to touch others you will open up a whole new arena of communication and relationships simply because you took the time to reach out.

Women are usually thought of as being more open

93

to touching others. Guys grow up with the idea that it isn't good for boys to express emotion through touch. I have a tragic memory of walking out of my kindergarten class innocently holding my friend's hand. (I was only five years old.) His father came rushing over to us with rage in his eyes and harshly broke apart our hands and in a brisk voice said, "Don't ever hold hands again! I don't want others to think my son is a homosexual!" As you can imagine I was devastated. I had no idea what the father meant but that didn't really matter; at the time all I knew was that there was something terribly wrong about touching other guys. (I already knew I would get cooties if I touched girls.)

It is healthy to touch others with a hug or even with a handshake. Recently I was speaking at a large high school camp where I had never seen a group of students who were more afraid of any type of physical contact. I began to challenge them to use this great form of communication. I told the guys that one way they can show that they care for each other (since guys feel uncomfortable hugging) is by a playful punch in the arm. After I was done speaking the guys got together and stood outside the door and formed a punching line. As I walked out I got mauled. By the time the camp was over, I left with many bruises, but I also left a changed group of students who realized the power of touch and the special message that it communicates.

Daily you will find ways in which you can touch others: passing through a group and putting a hand on a shoulder as you go by, walking by a friend and lightly grabbing his or her arm, extending an arm to a friend, a handshake, a hug, a high five or even a playful punch in the arm.

Now I am not challenging you to hang all over others or invade their privacy. But I do want you to understand that touching is needed and that it's a good way to communicate nonverbally.

Remember the challenge that Jesus gave us, "others will know that you are my disciples (Christians) by the way in which you *show* love for one another." I hope you have learned the importance and the challenge that nonverbal communication brings to us. In your attempt to not be a goon, try to make what you don't say show your love loud and clear.

Note

1. Freda S. Sathre-Eldon, *Let's Talk* (Glenview: Scott, Foresman and Company, 1981), p. 56.

MEEKNESS

Gentle and Strong

When I think of the word *meekness* I can think of only a few people who exemplify this quality. I think of Mother Teresa, Moses, and our Lord Jesus Christ as rare examples of people who demonstrate this precious quality. I once heard the term meek used to describe a tamed stallion. A wild, powerful and strong horse that is gentle enough for a child to pet.

The Bible often uses the word meek with the word humility. Nowhere in Scripture does meekness have a negative meaning. The meek are mighty in God's eyes as is illustrated in the Bible passage complimenting Moses on his character: "Now the man Moses was very meek, more than all men that were on the face of the earth" (Num. 12:3, *RSV*).

Jesus is a perfect example of a man who has the quality of meekness in His life. His gentleness is seen when He gathered the children together and put them in His arms and blessed them (see Mark 10:13-16).

Yet at another time in Jesus' life when He entered the Temple in Jerusalem and saw something similar to a swap meet going on He showed His anger and strength. There were people selling animals for sacrifices and money changers charging outrageous rates of interest. Jesus' reaction was to chase the irreverent crowd out of the Temple with a whip. He angrily turned over their tables and yelled at them to not make His Father's house into a market (see John 2:13-16).

These examples provide two extreme sides of Jesus'

personality. Yet they both help illustrate how diverse the personality of a meek person can be.

WHAT IS MEEKNESS?

It Is Not Weakness

For the longest time I associated meekness with weakness. I thought that if I was going to be meek I would turn into a spineless person who didn't have any opinions, couldn't speak in front of others, and didn't have fun. I found this to be all wrong as I followed my meek friends and studied the life of Christ. Christ spoke His message in front of thousands, had the power and authority to heal people, raised others from the dead, and was a leader of many. Yet He was meek.

Sensitivity is another branch of meekness that is often viewed as weakness. Young men are encouraged to not express any emotion or feelings. When they begin to cry they are told, "Big boys don't cry, so stop crying." As a result, many guys grow up having a hard time expressing their feelings. They repress their tears because "big boys don't cry." They may even believe that it's not macho to show pity and concern.

What the macho, insensitive male doesn't realize is that most women would rather have a sensitive man than a macho man. Most women relate better and feel that they are treated better by sensitive guys. People who are sensitive are able to be more affirming and seem to have a more Christlike concern for others.

It Is Humility

Being humble means being able to put other people before yourself. Someone who is humble enjoys being the "behind the scenes" person. They don't crave the spotlight of attention. The humble person receives a true sense of joy from seeing other people receive attention. As a matter of fact, a truly humble person will help others receive attention without taking any credit.

I am often impressed when I hear professional athletes take the spotlight off themselves and give other players or their team credit for their performance. That is humility in action.

Jesus used the small child as an example of humility because children have pure hearts. Jesus said, "Unless you change and become like little children, you will never enter the kingdom of heaven. Therefore, whoever humbles himself like this child is the greatest in the kingdom of heaven" (Matt. 18:3,4).

It Is Servanthood

Servanthood is another form of humility. An entire book could be written on this quality. Jesus said that He came not to be served but to serve and to give His life as a ransom for many (see Mark 10:45). Jesus is the ultimate example of servanthood not only for the many acts of service that He cheerfully did but also for giving His life so that we might live eternally. You can bet that people who possess the quality of meekness are among the greatest of servants.

It Is Gentleness

People who are meek seem to have a certain gentle, quiet spirit. They usually aren't loud, obnoxious, or rude. But they have a real peace about them. There is real beauty in this gentle quietness. Their actions are gentle and caring. They don't force their opinion on others but are usually asked their opinion because they speak with such wisdom.

Christ's gentleness is seen in the portrayal of His lifestyle. The apostle Paul used Christ as an example when he said, "By the meekness and gentleness of Christ, I appeal to you" (2 Cor. 10:1,2). May your gentleness be a reflection of your life in Christ.

MAKING MEEKNESS WORK

Be Slow to Speak

This is a tough one for me. I want to make sure that others hear my opinion. I usually sit at the edge of my seat so that I can put my bits of wisdom into the conversation. Meek people are in control of their tongues and conversation. They usually think before they speak so that their words will have meaning. Meek people are usually good listeners (remember the nonverbal communication chapter?) who are interested in the person as well as the content of the message.

James said in his letter, "My dear brothers, take note of this: Everyone should be quick to listen, slow to speak and slow to become angry" (Jas. 1:19).

The next time you are involved in a conversation with a group, sit back and observe the other people as well as the direction of the dialogue. Pray for the people that are speaking and even ask God to guide your words so that if you do speak you will speak with wisdom. (Read the second chapter of Proverbs for more information on how God desires for us to have wisdom.)

Put Others Before Yourself

Putting others first sounds like such a simple rule,

yet it is very difficult to put into practice. Our meek friends are servants. They are able to put others before themselves. This is an attitude Christ tried to teach His disciples before He returned to His Father.

In the book of John there is a beautiful description of Christ walking around the table, washing the disciples' feet. Christ explained why He humbled Himself in such a manner, "If I then, your Lord and Teacher (Master), have washed your feet, you ought—it is your duty, you are under obligation, you owe it—to wash one another's feet. For I have given you this as an example, so that you should do [in your turn] what I have done to you (John 13:14,15, *AMP.*). Christ showed He was a servant by putting others first.

Being a servant is a response to our faith in Christ. We don't serve looking for a reward or to be admired. We serve because we love God and because we see Christ's example and are challenged to imitate Him.

Meek people serve in small ways as well as large. They are the first ones to volunteer when asked, and even when they are not working on a particular project, they serve in other ways. They don't race to be first in line; they sit in the back seat of the car; they pick up litter that you and I walk over; they bring in the neighbor's trash cans; they give up their seats so another can have one; and they wait in line to buy tickets for everyone else while they play around. This isn't all a servant does but it gives you a good idea of some of the smaller ways in which meek people serve. But the interesting thing about these small ways of serving is that each one of us can do it. If you're like me you need to start with the small forms of servanthood and slowly work into making serving a part of your life-style. By doing this we will

103

be strengthened in our pursuit of meekness.

Realize How Great God Is

The Bible speaks of fearing God. This doesn't mean that we should be afraid of Him but that we should be in awe of Him. When we understand how awesome God is we will be able to see ourselves in a better perspective.

One of the things that keeps us from being meek is that we have an overly inflated idea of who we are. But the fact is: we are nothing compared to God. We need to have the attitude of David the psalmist who praised God for His greatness and majesty and at the same time considered himself a worm. But God doesn't treat us like worms even though that's what we are in comparison to Him.

A meek person realizes that he or she is nothing before God. It is only because of God's grace (undeserved favor) that we have life with Him. We are new creations in Christ. The old creation was lost when you came to Jesus. God is in the process of making you into the image of Christ (see 2 Cor. 5:13-20). When you really understand this you will realize that the beautiful, sensitive, humble quality of meekness comes from knowing that God has the power and love to make you His new creation.

CLIQUES

Why You Should Become a Clique Buster

Cliques are everywhere! Some people believe that cliques exist only in the church. Students in my area seem to think that they are only in our youth group. But the fact is, cliques begin in preschool and continue through life into adult society. Cliques surround us, frustrate us, and can make our lives miserable.

A clique can be defined as a group of people who aren't interested in including new people in their group. You can probably think of examples of cliques in your neighborhood, church, school and work place. Becoming part of a clique is oftentimes not something we do consciously. It may simply be the progressive process of those friendships in which we stay without welcoming new members. Once we are conscious that we are part of a clique, we need to learn how to respond appropriately.

After hearing the following song I realized that I needed to do something about the cliques I was involved in. Read these words carefully. I pray that you might be sensitized to those waiting outside your group.

Elaine lives on the bad side of town.
    Nothing goes on there, it only goes down
Her family is a sad situation
    and she's the victim of their frustration

Down the street at the church it's a different
    world
    Wednesday night and Sunday
The Christians there could really help that girl
    if only they would say

(Chorus)
COME ON ELAINE
    COME ON ELAINE
COME ON ELAINE
    Let's get together
COME ON ELAINE
    Oh Elaine
COME ON ELAINE
    We'll try to make it better (for you)

At her school nobody knows she's there
    except to laugh at how she does her hair
She ain't got money for the Sassoon jeans
    She don't know how to play the video
    machines
Well at the church there's a girl who could
    reach her
    but it's kinda out of her way
Her choice of friends is her finest feature
    and she's too cool to say

(Chorus)

We'll try to make it better for you
    You need to know somebody cares for you
Someone to help with what you're going
    through
    and share the love of Jesus with you[1]

108

WHAT CLIQUES CAN DO

Cliques Make Your Youth Group Look Bad

When someone new walks into your youth group do they feel loved and accepted? People need to feel acceptance or they won't stay or get involved.

I can think of very few times when someone new to my youth group has introduced himself to me and asked how he could get involved. The norm is for people to visit and wait to see if they are greeted and accepted. If the group is friendly, it is easier for them to get involved. But if they aren't welcomed, they lose interest and usually leave with bad feelings. A group may have a bunch of great people, but if they are not friendly to others outside their group, they aren't going to earn or deserve a good reputation.

Cliques Alienate People

Growing up I was involved with a group of friends from my church who became very close. Many of these friends were eventually in full time Christian service; this was one of the many things we shared in addition to just liking each other.

We referred to ourselves as the "gang." As time went by and we began to spread out into various cities we started calling ourselves the "Orange Gang" because we all came from the city of Orange, California.

Something very interesting happened as some of us began to get involved in serious relationships outside of the gang. We had built such a strong bond of friendship within our tight little group that it became difficult for our new girlfriends and boyfriends to feel comfortable when the gang was together. I was totally unaware that

109

these new people felt so badly until I met Cathy and she began to tell me about her feelings. Others who had come in from the outside had similar feelings. The gang didn't try to be mean, we were just comfortable and happy and didn't make a big enough effort to welcome newcomers. No group, not even a group of ministers, is immune to becoming a clique.

It is obvious that if someone doesn't feel accepted, they are going to feel alienated. Those of us who have felt like we don't belong know that to feel unwanted is horrible. Even if we know that God loves us unconditionally, we still have a hard time feeling wanted when we aren't allowed to become part of a group. Sadder still is the fact that this type of alienation takes place in the church. The church should be the last place on the face of the earth where people should feel unwanted and unwelcomed.

Acceptance of others should be a response to the obedience and love that you have for God. When Paul wrote to the church in Phillipi he said, "My prayer for you is that you will overflow more and more with love for others" (Phil. 1:9, *TLB*). Paul's words should challenge you and your group as you open up to love others.

Cliques Ruin God's Plan for Reaching Others

One of the ways in which God has chosen to reach those that don't know Christ is through His Church. But when the Church doesn't accept outsiders it becomes a Christian club. If God wanted us to have a Christian club He would have taken us up to heaven so we could be exclusively with other Christians. But God chose differently. He wants His Church to welcome those that don't know Him.

110

Throughout the New Testament there is an appeal to preach to those outside the Church the message that Christ died for our sins. If we are to take God's Word seriously then we need to open our lives, our churches, and our youth groups to others. We can't afford to have cliques if we are to effectively live out God's plan.

HOW TO BECOME A CLIQUE BUSTER

Start with Another Person

Once you have decided that you need to make some changes it is important for you to sell someone else on the idea of breaking up cliques. Explain how dangerous cliques can become and ask if he or she is willing to help you become a clique buster. It is easier to do with another person helping and supporting you.

Develop a strategy, decide who you should talk to, and what cliques are most corruptive. Take people aside one by one and ask them for their help and understanding as you work to break up cliques.

Bring People into Your Group

Many of us learn by example. This may be an example of a time when you need to set a standard for your group. In a loving, rather than cocky or pious manner, begin reaching out to new people; watch for them, greet them, and invite them to become a part of your group. Open up to outsiders. Begin spending time with them and make it a point to try to incorporate them into the life of your group. In a very real sense you can become a pastor to outsiders. This doesn't mean that you give up all your old friends but that you make new friends a part of your old friends.

111

Other cliques will be exposed to what you are trying to do and hopefully they will catch the vision and want to become involved in clique busting.

Pray for Sensitivity

This is the most important step in becoming a clique buster. I learned this from my wife Cathy. Before every program, meeting, or party she prays that God will make her sensitive to the needs of those with whom she will come in contact. It's amazing, but most of the time God directs her to people who are on the outside of the group and are feeling uncomfortable.

Every time you enter a situation where there may be outsiders pretend to put on "sensitive glasses" and ask God that He might be the lens to help you see where you can best be used.

If after reading this chapter you don't think that there is a need in your group for a clique buster, you are either involved in an unusual group of people who are very sensitive, or you aren't looking very hard. Remember, non-Christians judge Christianity by the way Christians show love for one another. Keep this in mind as you set out to be a clique buster.

Note

1. COME ON ELAINE by Rob Frazier
   © Copyright 1984 by LIBRIS MUSIC (A DIV. OF LEXICON MUSIC, INC.) ASCAP All rights reserved. International copyright secured. Used by permission.

LAUGHTER

Add Joy to Your Life

This will be a fun chapter to read! It's not a funny chapter, but one that will give you something fun and exciting to think about. My purpose isn't to make you a comedian, but to present a few of the many reasons why it is good to laugh. Then I'll give you a few ideas on how you can develop a better sense of humor.

Let me begin by saying that there isn't a great deal about laughter in the Bible. There aren't verses that say, "Thou shall laugh." We don't have any accounts of Jesus cracking jokes to His disciples. Nor do we have record of Jesus saying, "I want to teach you how to make others laugh so that when I am gone there will still be laughter in the world." But just because Jesus didn't instruct us directly to laugh doesn't mean that He didn't laugh.

Jesus is always pictured in religious movies as being so serious and as speaking in such an intense, deep voice that He appears angelic and non-human. But since Jesus was human, I'm sure He laughed. Just think of the people and the situations that surrounded Him. Imagine the look on the face of the guy who was carrying the jug of water when Jesus turned it into wine (see John 2). Or the reaction of the crowd when four guys had the guts to lower their buddy through the roof of the house where Jesus was preaching (see Mark 2). There are many stories in the Bible that are just plain funny if we consider how we would feel if they were happening here and now.

Even though the Bible says little directly about laughter, it does cover the topic indirectly. The writer of Proverbs said, "A *cheerful* heart is a good medicine, but a downcast spirit dries up the bones" (17:22, *RSV*, emphasis added).

A word used in the Bible that has a similar meaning to the word cheerful is the word *joy*. The Bible has numerous verses that speak of joy and gladness in the same breath.

When I think of the word joy I think of happiness, good times, and laughter. Joy in your life can bring about the needed response of laughter. It is much easier to be a person who uses and appreciates laughter when there is joy in your life.

Unless you like to be unhappy, laughter should be a treat for you. Try reading the rest of this chapter with an open mind, a smile on your face, and a chuckle in your heart.

WHY IT'S GOOD TO LAUGH

Laughter Helps Bring Joy into the Lives of Others

People who love to laugh are some of the most joyful people I know. One of my favorite things is to be with friends, laughing and having a good time.

When I was in college I used to look forward to Thursday nights with great anticipation. On Thursday nights I would go to a restaurant, meet a friend, drink gallons of ice tea, and talk and laugh until the early hours of the morning. The reason that I loved this time so much is that it brought joy into my life during a par-

116

ticularly stressful time. Many days during college it seemed like I moved from stress to stress to rush to study to exhaustion. I really needed a shot in the arm of laughter.

There are many people in the world today who are practicing being unhappy. They look for the bad and pass on all the good. Instead of having joyful heart they have a depressed heart. I see people like this all the time. Some of them are in my youth group. But amazingly, laughter can almost magically bring joy to even a depressed heart.

Laugher Makes People Feel Comfortable

There are times in our lives when we are in a tense situation and all of a sudden the tension is broken by laughter. We feel so much better! This happens to me when I walk in the dark. I'm afraid of the dark (don't look so smug; you probably are too). When I enter a dark room I want to get the lights on right away. In the meantime I use laughter as my flashlight. As I'm searching for the light switch and feeling tense, I force myself to laugh so I won't be so scared. It really works!

There may be times when a person entering your youth group or classroom for the first time is incredibly uncomfortable. This is not only a good time to meet a new person, it may also be a great time to lighten the tension with some laughter. "It's good to meet you. This room may look and smell like a locker room, but it's really a great place to be" or "Oh, you go to University High School, that's great. We've needed some quality people in this group for some time now." As long as you do not use put-downs or embarrass a newcomer, light humor can make the new person feel good about the

117

comfortable atmosphere and can help make a good first impression.

There are some exceptions to this rule! Recently, Cathy and I were going to the house of one of my old high school friends for a party, a sort of reunion. Cathy knew very few people and naturally felt uncomfortable. We were met at the door by a friend of mine. This friend immediately launched into a rude, gross joke. He thought it was really funny. The only problem was that he was the only one who laughed. We obviously felt uncomfortable, which made him uneasy, and the rest of the evening was awkward.

It helps to use tasteful and affirming humor when you try to make others feel comfortable.

Laughter Can Make People Feel Better Physically

There have been many studies published lately that indicate that laughing can be good for your health. There's an old story of a doctor who said, "If you can't take a joke then you'll have to take medicine."

One man, Norman Cousins, has written a best-selling book, *Anatomy of an Illness,* about how laughter cured him of an incurable form of spinal arthritis. It's a remarkable story!

You may even find that you will feel healthier if you will let laughter provide you with a release from your tension. Dr. James J. Walsh in his book *Laughter and Health* says that laughter provides a much needed massaging of the lungs, heart, liver, pancreas and intestines.

Now I don't advise you to read *Mad* magazine and watch comedies instead of going to the doctor, but it is good to know that laughter can have a positive effect on your body.

118

Laughter Helps Others Hear You
When You Talk About God

When I speak at a camp or to a school group I like to begin with a funny story that relates to my topic or with something else that will make my audience laugh. People are always thinking, consciously or subconsciously, "Why should I listen to you?" I try to keep this in mind when I get the chance to speak. I need to earn the right to be heard.

Last month at a convention I heard five people speak for 30 minutes each. Back to back. You should have seen the audience perk up when someone told a funny story or a good joke. It was as if someone had shocked them.

My response to a humorous story is, "That was funny. I like this person. I wonder what she has to say." I am more interested in listening to her now that she has won the right to be heard. This is effective communication.

In the book, *Secrets of Successful Humor,* the authors give seven reasons why laughter works with both individuals and with audiences.

1. It is one of the most effective forms of emotional communication.
2. It can dissolve tension in people to whom you are relating and can help them relax.
3. It can help you gain and keep your listeners' attention.
4. It can increase your credibility (earning the right to be heard) and help you come across as a real person.

119

5. It can help overcome resistance to points you are trying to make.
6. It can provide needed breaks in a conversation or speech.
7. It can help drive home a point.

These points are important to keep in mind when you are speaking to others. If we take the importance of sharing the Good News of Jesus Christ seriously, we need to be the best possible communicators that we can be. I'm not saying that we all need to be great public speakers, but I am saying that we need to know how humor can help us communicate the life-changing message of Christ.

Along with a better understanding of what laughter can do for us, we need to learn a few ways in which we can develop a better sense of humor.

DEVELOPING A SENSE OF HUMOR

Realize That Laughing Doesn't Expose Weakness

Some people choose not to laugh because they feel that laughing makes them seem weak. Wanting to portray a tough, macho image, they view laughter as a sign of weakness and vulnerability. Often the only time these people laugh is when they see something that is damaging or hurtful. The truth is that people like this need laughter more than anyone else. Behind their tough masks is the same desire for joy and happiness that you and I have.

I have found in counseling these macho types that they are really people searching for acceptance and happy relationships. They just don't know how to go about it. They have learned to relate to other people in a negative manner. And unfortunately, they haven't given themselves the freedom to enjoy life and laughter.

If you fit this description, you need to realize that laughter is one quality source of joy that you need in order to move down the road to happiness.

Laugh at the Little Things in Life

In developing a sense of humor it is important to be on the lookout for amusing situations. Many funny things happen around us each day. But often they are viewed as just another source of stress or as being simply uncomfortable situations. In reality these situations might be very funny.

An example of what I mean is what I call "unmentioned commonalities." These are things that happen all the time but we never talk about them and we rarely even notice when they happen to someone else. For instance, have you ever noticed that when a person trips while he is walking he will inevitably look back to see what it was that he tripped over as if to say, "Who did that to me?"

Another of the unmentioned commonalities is that for some reason everyone takes bread from the middle of the loaf. They just reach right in the bag to the middle as if the first couple of pieces had something wrong with them.

Or how about the uncomfortable situation when sitting at a table and your foot touches another foot. You think to yourself, "How can I move my foot without her realizing that we were touching?"

These are the little common things that happen to

121

everyone. They can be very funny if they are viewed in the right way.

Listening to comedians can help a person understand how to make little things funny. If you ever get the chance to listen to a Bill Cosby record, don't pass it up. His humor is brilliant! He takes the little, ordinary things in life and makes them come alive because he finds a way to see humor in them. He makes sitting in a dentist's chair humorous (I view the same chair as a curse from God).

Gifts can be funny. I just received three new pairs of colored socks (funny in itself when I remember what I thought of colored socks when I was in high school) from my mother-in-law. They came on a plastic hanger. Now what is that hanger used for? Is there such a thing as a little sock closet where you hang your socks up instead of rolling or folding them? To me, a sock hanger is pretty funny (but then remember, I *wear* colored socks).

Laugh At Yourself

One of the greatest tragedies of modern times is that many people take life far too seriously. They forget to laugh and love. They are so concerned about building their mountain of personal credentials that they forget about the mud puddle at the bottom that they need to play in to maintain their sanity.

When I take myself too seriously, trying to make myself look good, I usually end up doing something or saying something really stupid. Jesus said, "For every one who exalts himself will be humbled, and he who humbles himself will be exalted" (Luke 14:11, *RSV*). Jesus also told His followers to become childlike; little children aren't as concerned with making themselves look good as we are.

Tim Hansel has some wise comments about taking ourselves too seriously: "The problems with taking ourselves too seriously are countless. Afraid to fail, we no longer risk. Afraid someone will see behind our image, we no longer share. Afraid that we will appear to need help, we can no longer be vulnerable . . . . We withdraw into a petty world consumed in emptiness and fear . . . in our fear of becoming childlike, in our fear of becoming a fool for Christ, in our fear of being seen as we are, we discover all too late that it's impossible to be fully human and fully alive."[1]

One thing that I do in my attempt to not take myself too seriously is to carry a picture of myself that is so ridiculous looking that I have to laugh each time I see it. I realize that there is no way I can take myself seriously when I have the potential of looking that funny. I would make a great circus clown!

I have a friend who is overweight and who actually makes fat jokes about himself. He figures that if he doesn't, somebody else will. He would rather laugh at himself than be laughed at. This helps him to see past his problem and to attempt to become the person God wants him to be.

If you are too concerned with how you look you might want to ask yourself, "Am I worrying so much about myself that I'm not listening to God? If God wanted to use me for something great, would I hear Him?"

The apostle Paul understood that if he took himself too seriously he would end up being disappointed because of his human weakness. He said, "Now I am glad to boast about how weak I am; I am glad to be a living demonstration of Christ's power, instead of showing off my own power and abilities. Since I know it is all for Christ's good . . . for when I am weak, then I am strong—the less I have, the more I depend on Him" (2 Cor. 12:9,10, *TLB*).

If you can learn to laugh at yourself in spite of your weakness, then you are on your way to developing a great sense of humor.

Laughter can be very much like tears because it is an emotional release. If this emotion is used in a positive manner, it can become one of your greatest sources of happiness and overflowing joy. Keep laughing!

Note

1. Tim Hansel, *When I Relax I Feel Guilty* (Elgin: David C. Cook Publishing Co., 1979), p. 87.

REFLECTION

Taking Time to Know God
and Yourself

If you have read this far there is a good chance that you aren't as big of a goon as you were when you first started reading the book. This last chapter is the final link in the chain of not being a goon.

As you look around at the people with whom you interact each day you will see a number of individuals who look as though they are always lost. They run around moving from one thing to another trying to find the best deal, trying to make a deal, or trying to be in on a deal. They seem driven by the illusion that being busy is good. But the fact is that busy is not always good.

I'm slowly learning this lesson and it's not an easy one for me to learn. My friend Doug Webster has been challenging me to keep asking myself this question, "Why am I doing what I'm doing?"

Many of us like to please people and we will do almost anything to be people pleasers. I know of many families who have gone through the tragedy of divorce because work and being busy was more important than the marriage and working on the relationships within the family.

Doug has helped me to see that when I am busy and my schedule is out of control I begin to lose sight of my relationship with God. Usually when a Christian gets really busy the first thing that is sacrificed is his or her time with God.

The challenge in this chapter is for you to see that God created rest and that rest is both good and needed.

Without it there is little time for reflection and the many great benefits that we receive when we reflect on God.

God Created Rest

The Bible tells us, "By the seventh day God had finished the work he had been doing; so on the seventh day he rested from all his work. And God blessed the seventh day and made it holy, because on it he rested from all the work of creating that he had done" (Gen. 2:2,3). God didn't need to rest, because He is God. But He chose to rest so that we would see His pattern and observe it.

Resting gives us time to reflect on what we have been doing. It also offers refreshment from all of the activity we have been involved in.

Even Jesus Rested

We find that the Lord Jesus rested on various occasions. He only had a few years of ministry on earth and yet He took time to reflect on what He had been doing and to communicate with His Father.

I would think that Jesus would want to do all that He could and spend all of His waking hours ministering to and healing people. Yet Jesus didn't do this. Jesus was the source of rest yet He took needed rest time from His busy schedule (see Mark 6:46b,47).

WHEN WE ARE TOO BUSY

We Miss Out on the Small Things in Life

Our society usually equates big with beautiful but some of the most beautiful things on this great planet are small. When we get busy we tend to pass the small things by without much thought. Before I was married I had the opportunity to live in a large beach house that was 15 feet from the bay. Every morning I woke up to the stillness of the bay as it stretched out past the jetty and into the ocean. Boats, birds and jumping fish would regularly be on patrol and I would watch them from my bedroom window. It was a beautiful sight but the longer I lived there the less I cared about this special scenery. It wasn't until Cathy and I got married and moved into a small apartment in the middle of the city that I began to miss the small beauties of the ocean bay. I'm glad that it didn't take me longer to notice that the small things in this world are both beautiful and important.

This poem, written by an anonymous friar in a monastery late in his life, seems to say exactly what I mean:

> If I had my life to live over again, I'd try to make more mistakes next time.
> I would relax, I would limber up, I would be sillier than I have been this trip.
> I know of very few things I would take seriously.
> I would take more trips. I would be crazier.
> I would climb more mountains, swim more rivers, and watch more sunsets.
> I would do more walking and looking.
> I would eat more ice cream and less beans.
> I would have more actual troubles, and fewer imaginary ones.
> You see, I'm one of those people who lives life prophylactically and sensibly hour after hour, day after day. I've been one of those

people who never go anywhere without a
thermometer, a hot-water bottle, a gargle, a
raincoat, aspirin, and a parachute.
If I had to do it over again I would go places,
do things, and travel lighter than I have.
If I had my life to live over I would start bare-
footed earlier in the spring and stay that
way later in the fall.
I would play hookey more.
I wouldn't make such good grades, except by
accident.
I would ride on more merry-go-rounds.
I'd pick more daisies.[1]

May this poem be a challenge for you to slow down
and see and experience some of the small things God
has given us.

We Miss Out on Knowing Ourselves

We desperately need time alone to reflect on where
we have been and how we have interacted with our
world. We need to evaluate our actions and ask questions about the situations we have been in to see if we
really did the right thing. In this way we can learn from
our victories as well as from our failures. Finding out
who we really are takes time. Like any discipline, if you
want to be a good person you have got to practice; you
must set aside time to reflect.

I use the time as I drive to work or from one place to
another to get in touch with my inner self. And I have
found that as this has become my habit, I really look forward to driving. I used to hate to drive until I gave this

time to myself to think and reflect on where I have been, my feelings, my relationship with God, with Cathy, and with others. When do you take time to be by yourself and reflect on who you really are?

We Miss Out on Knowing God

God wants to spend time with us and yet when we don't take time to reflect on who He is and how He is active in our lives we tend to lose the closeness that we should experience with Him. We settle for second best and we give Him second best. The following statement describes how one person felt about this tendency to miss out on a relationship with God:

> I would like to buy $3 worth of God, please, not enough to explode my soul or disturb my sleep, but just enough to equal a cup of warm milk or a snooze in the sunshine. I don't want enough of Him to make me love a black man or pick beets with a migrant. I want ecstasy, not transformation; I want the warmth of the womb, not a new birth. I want a pound of the eternal in a paper sack. I would like to buy $3 worth of God, please.[2]

The psalmist wrote the following about God: "Be still, and know that I am God" (Ps. 46:10). Another translation reads, "Stand silent! Know that I am God" *(TLB)*. If you aren't setting aside a quiet time to get to know God there's a good chance that you are asking for only three dollars worth of Him. Be challenged to spend quiet time with God knowing that He looks forward to this time to become close and to refresh you.

131

PRACTICAL SUGGESTIONS FOR REFLECTION

Find a Quiet Spot

So often we are surrounded by music, television, and other distracting noises that make it difficult to enjoy quietness. Find a spot in or near your house that you know will be quiet and that you can retreat to for time to reflect. Use this time to be quiet and listen for God to speak to you in your heart and thoughts.

A few summers ago I was in Danville, California and I found an abandoned tree swing. I would retreat to that swing when I needed to be alone. To this day when I visit Danville I go back to that swing because of the great memories I have of the time spent there with God.

Start a Journal

Find any type of folder and begin to write down the thoughts, dreams, fantasies, and goals you think of during your time alone. I use a cheap 40-page spiral notebook so I can buy a new one every other month and because it makes me feel like I have room to write a lot. Here are two entries that I wrote recently:

Nov. 8th: Today I felt like the only time that God was in my life was when I drove by the church. I had a lousy day, God. I really want to please you and be the person that you want me to be but I'm struggling with who I am and my communication with you . . . sorry. I love you though, Doug.

Nov. 13th: This morning I feel great about myself! I got good sleep and after playing an hour of basketball I feel real good. I know this is going to be a great day. God, teach me something new today and make me sensitive to those that I come in contact with. Thanks God for my body and the abilities that you have given me. Forgive me when I often take these things for granted. Thanks for loving me!

You have the freedom to write whatever you would like. No one else needs to see what you write. I try to write more of my feelings and thoughts than about what I did today. Then I go back once a month and reflect on where I have been, how I have grown, and what I have been through.

Don't be intimidated by rules or guidelines to writing; just write whatever you want to. Let this be your time to freely reflect on you and your God.

Solos

A solo is a time when you are going away to be by yourself for a specific period of time. I was introduced to this concept on a houseboat camp when I was a sophomore in high school. Our group was dropped off on the land to spend six hours by ourselves without talking to anyone or listening to the radio. My initial reaction was "You've got to be kidding. I could never do that!" But to my surprise, and everyone else's, this experience turned out to be the favorite event of the camp. Our group loved it! Many of the people who experienced the solo still incorporate that discipline in their lives today. Give it a try.

Creative Times with God

Who says that your time with God has to be the same every day? I know many people get tired of trying to read their Bibles every day. They begin to feel guilty, and then they stop reading it all together. But even if you don't read your Bible everyday, you should have daily time with God. Why not make your time with God a creative experience? Write Him a letter; think of ways in which He reminds you of something in your room; go outside and look around at His creation and thank Him for it; paraphrase a story out of the Bible; or write out your favorite verse and tell God why you like it. The options are limitless. God wants you to spend time with Him and He would rather have that time be creative than none at all.

My prayer is that you would spend some time in reflection on all that you have learned in this book and ask God to begin to change you into His image. Reflect on how you can put into practice some of these qualities in your life in an attempt to be the person God created you to be. Remember, God loves you not for what you do but for who you are.

There are many goons out there living life in a "human costume." These people need to personally know our Lord Jesus and begin the process of change. Share a little of what you have learned with those in your world and help them know there's more to life than being a goon.

May the words that Doug Webster spoke to me during a time of personal stress and busyness challenge you to learn to be still and know your God.

Reduce and master; don't take yourself so seriously. Laugh more, pursue God's love, enjoy people and wear your underwear over your clothes.

Notes

1. Tim Hansel, *When I Relax I Feel Guilty* (Elgin: David C. Cook Publishing Co., 1979), p. 44, 45.
2. Charles Swindoll, *Improving Your Serve: The Art of Unselfish Living* (Waco: Word Books, 1981), p. 29.